Making Americans, Remaking America

Dilemmas in American Politics

Series Editor **L. Sandy Maisel,** *Colby College*

Dilemmas in American Politics offers teachers and students a series of quality books on timely topics and key institutions in American government. Each text will examine a "real world" dilemma and will be structured to cover the historical, theoretical, policy relevant, and future dimensions of its subject.

BOOKS IN THIS SERIES

Making Americans, Remaking America

Immigration and
Immigrant Policy

Louis DeSipio
University of Illinois at Urbana-Champaign

Rodolfo O. de la Garza
University of Texas at Austin

Westview Press
A Member of the Perseus Books Group

Dilemmas in American Politics

Copyright © 1998 by Westview Press, A Member of the Perseus Books Group

Published in 1998 in the United States of America by Westview Press, 5500 Central Avenue, Boulder, Colorado 80301-2877, and in the United Kingdom by Westview Press, 12 Hid's Copse Road, Cumnor Hill, Oxford OX2 9JJ

Library of Congress Cataloging-in-Publication Data
DeSipio, Louis.
  Making Americans, remaking America : immigration and immigrant
policy / Louis DeSipio, Rodolfo O. de la Garza.
    p.   cm. — (Dilemmas in American politics)
  Includes bibliographical references and index.
  ISBN 0-8133-1943-9 (hardcover). — ISBN 0-8133-1944-7 (pbk.)
  1. Immigrants—United States.   2. United States—Emigration and
immigration.   3. United States—Emigration and immigration—
Government policy.   4. Naturalization—United States.   I. De la
Garza, Rudolfo O.   II. Title.   III. Series.
JV6465.D47   1998
325.73—dc21   98-10675
                                                                        CIP

The paper used in this publication meets the requirements of the American National Standard for Permanence of Paper for Printed Library Materials Z39.48-1984.

10   9   8   7   6   5   4   3   2

To our immigrant heritage

Luigi Ricca, great-grandfather
Clara Richieda, great-grandmother
Gioachino DeSipio, grandfather
Italians by birth

Laurence Walton, great-great-great-great-grandfather
English by birth

Sofia Oropeza, mother
Mexican by birth

Adelaida Traveria, mother-in-law
Serafin Corbelle, father-in-law
Ileana Corbelle, wife
Cubans by birth

and others unknown
Americans by choice

Contents

4 Immigrants and Natives: Rights, Responsibilities, and Interaction   93

5 Immigrants Versus Immigration: Structuring the Discussion of Dilemmas in Immigration, Naturalization, and Settlement Policy   125

Tables and Illustrations

Tables

Illustrations

1

A Nation of Immigrants: Continuing Dilemmas

On January 30, 1996, a rumor swept New York City's undocumented immigrant community. The Immigration and Naturalization Service (INS), the rumor reported, was giving away "green cards," the immigrant visas that offer immigrants the opportunity to live and work permanently in the United States and, after five years, to be eligible for U.S. citizenship. The rumor was false. Yet in the first few hours after the rumor began to spread, over one thousand undocumented immigrants braved the nighttime winter chill to travel to the INS to wait in line for the visas that never were.

Ironically, the source of the rumor was not himself an undocumented immigrant. Instead, he was New York's mayor, Rudolph Giuliani. The day the rumor began, he had held a news conference to encourage undocumented immigrants and potential immigrants to apply by mail for a new program designed to diversify the flow of immigrants to the United States. Eventually, these applications would lead to a lottery that would result in the award of approximately forty thousand visas many months in the future to residents of countries that had not been the source of many recent immigrants to the United States. Congress designed this program to expand the range of countries supplying legal immigrants to the United States. Whatever Congress's motives, Mayor Giuliani's advice to immigrants abroad engendered a surge of hope among immigrants already in the United States.

Although the origin of this rumor was unique, the reaction should be of little surprise. Increasingly over the past thirty years, demand for U.S. immigrant visas has increased dramatically. People throughout the world seek the opportunity to migrate to the United States.

In fact, on the same day that Mayor Giuliani's entreaty was misunderstood, approximately 2,500 people immigrated to permanent residence nationwide, and 1,400 became U.S. citizens. These totals are estimates based on annual immigration of approximately 900,000 people and naturalization of approximately 500,000. Since many undocumented immigrants enter and leave the United States regularly for day labor or short-term work, it is harder to estimate a daily figure for undocumented immigration. The most rigorous estimates suggest that the number of undocumented immigrants in the United States increases by 300,000 per year. However, every month, the United States deports more than 5,000 un-

3

documented immigrants and permits 125,000 who have been arrested to depart voluntarily instead of facing formal deportation proceedings.

In this book, we examine U.S. immigration and naturalization policy and the policy choices that the polity has made regarding immigration and the settlement of immigrants. We look at the numbers of immigrants, the types of immigration, and how the flow of immigrants has changed over time. We also examine what happens to immigrants once they arrive in the United States, both formally, in terms of joining the polity as naturalized citizens, and informally, in terms of interacting with other populations in the United States and receiving different types of benefits based on their immigration or naturalization status. Our goal is to pinpoint the dilemmas that the United States faces in being a nation of immigrants that sets as a national ideal the political incorporation of these immigrants.

Terminology

Before we get too deeply into the questions of immigration, naturalization, and settlement, we want to explain some terms and concepts that will appear repeatedly in our discussion. A more complete glossary appears at the end of the book.

The beginning of the immigration process is a decision by an individual or a family to migrate. **Migration** is movement from one place to another. In the United States, we take migration largely for granted. People migrate from city to city or region to region for education, for employment, and often just for a change of scene. When migration—movement—crosses an international frontier, it is called by different names—**emigration** and **immigration**—though, at a fundamental level, it is also still migration. Emigration means leaving one country. Immigration refers to entering another.

Emigration and immigration are collective terms. Individuals who leave one country are emigrants. When they enter the new country, they become immigrants. In both cases, as well as when people move within a country, they are migrants.

Since emigration and immigration require that a migrant cross an international frontier, the migrant must usually get the permission of the country of origin, of the receiving country, or of both. Some countries restrict emigration. These countries do not want to lose the labor, skills, knowledge, experiences, or assets of potential emigrants. Some countries also restrict emigration for symbolic reasons; they do not want to give the appearance to other countries in the world that their subjects are not satisfied living in that country. Prior to its collapse, for example, the Soviet Union limited the emigration of Jews, among many other groups. Today, some countries charge a hefty tax for the issuance of an emigration visa to reduce the appeal of emigration. With the expansion of the world's transportation links and the development of international communications technology, controlling international emigration has become increasingly rare.

Although formal restrictions on emigration have diminished, the potential for migration is not equal from all parts of the world. Transportation links make migration easier from some parts of the world than others. Patterns of previous migration from a region increase the likelihood that new migrants will come from that same region. As we will indicate, migration is often not an individual act, so the previous immigration experiences of friends or family members shape where subsequent emigrants go and how they adapt to the receiving society. Finally, emigration is limited to those who can afford the cost of international transit and who have a reasonable expectation of being able to survive in the receiving country. Immigrants, unlike the common stereotype assigned them, are usually not the poorest of the poor in their sending countries. The poorest usually cannot afford the cost of migration or do not have the skills to find work in the receiving society. Instead, immigrants are usually relatively more successful members of the sending society.

Compared to emigration, immigration is much more highly restricted. Few countries accept large numbers of immigrants each year. Even fewer accept large numbers of immigrants with the promise that these immigrants can become full members of the receiving society. The four largest immigrant-receiving countries are Australia, Canada, New Zealand, and the United States. Each of these countries offers many of its immigrants the opportunity not just to live there permanently but also to join the country as a full member—as a **citizen**.

Each country sets its own standards for immigrants. Broadly, these standards involve three types of potential immigrants—those with blood ties, skills or wealth, or ideological congruence. The largest of these categories involves blood ties, whether immediate or fictive. Some countries look for individuals who are related to citizens of the receiving country. Others seek people who share a common ethnic background or a common religious background. The second category for immigrant admissions grants a higher likelihood of admission to people with specialized job skills or with wealth that can be transferred to the new country. Even countries that admit few immigrants rarely reject the wealthy seeking a new home, particularly when those wealthy immigrants are willing to invest their wealth. Although the truly rich are relatively few (and often not interested in migration), the educated and technically skilled make up a larger pool of potential migrants who are often welcomed as immigrants. The final category of people who are sometimes granted immigration eligibility are those in ideological agree-

ment with the leaders of the receiving state. As the salience of the world's dominant ideologies has declined, this category of potential immigrants has also declined. Nevertheless, for some countries it remains an explanatory factor for high-
profile immigrants.

Although the decision to migrate is individual, scholars have identified patterns
that explain why many people migrate. The simplest pattern is a supply and demand, or push and pull, model. Countries with high populations relative to the
jobs that are available, with political strife, starvation, or low wages for skilled oc-
cupations, tend to have high levels of emigration. By contrast, countries with labor shortages, political stability, high wages, and a willingness to admit immigrants experience immigration. In the modern world, governments shape this
flow by their tolerance for emigration and immigration. Private enterprise also
shapes the migrant flow by its patterns of labor recruitment.

In the United States, we identify immigrants who have entered the country
under the provisions of the immigration law as **permanent residents** (see Illustration 1.1). The name suggests a great deal about their status. They may remain
in the United States permanently under this status unless they give up their permanent residence by moving abroad for lengthy periods or by committing a
crime that results in their deportation. Although they may live out their lives as
permanent residents, after five years U.S. permanent residents have the option of
naturalizing as U.S. citizens. We discuss naturalization further later in this
section.

With immigration often restricted to family members, the rich, the skilled, or
ideologues, many potential immigrants are not eligible for formal or legal immigration. This leads to a second stream of international migrants, those who enter
a country *without* the legal authorization to remain permanently. In the United
States, we identify these immigrants as **illegal** or **undocumented immigrants** (the
term that we will use in this book).

As we will indicate, undocumented immigrants in the United States are hetero-
geneous. Some are family members of U.S. citizens or permanent residents. Others are people who have migrated to the United States to seek work opportunities.
Some of these work in unskilled or semiskilled positions that are shunned by U.S.
citizens, but others have advanced technical skills and work in positions desired
by American workers. Still other undocumented immigrants are fleeing political
persecution or economic privation in their home countries. Some crossed borders without legal permission, whereas others entered with legal but short-term
visas and stayed in the United States after the visa expired. Clearly, these categories of undocumented immigrants overlap. Economic or political persecution
in sending countries can encourage undocumented immigration that results in

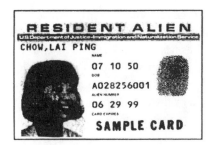

ILLUSTRATION 1.1   A Resident Alien Card, also known as a "Green Card"

work opportunities. The experiences of permanent residents and undocumented immigrants from one era lead to subsequent migration even though the conditions in the sending country change. Finally, as we will suggest, U.S. immigration policy often encourages undocumented immigration by allowing some family members to immigrate as permanent residents while denying other family members access to legal immigration.

As we have structured this discussion of international migration, the two categories of immigrants—permanent residents and undocumented immigrants— should describe all immigrants, since an immigrant is either in the receiving country with the permission of the receiving country or not. Alas, the structure of immigration is much more complex.

Some countries admit immigrants solely for labor-related reasons. Immigrants are permitted to stay in the receiving country only as long as they perform the job that spurred their entry and as long as the receiving society needs their labor. Between 1943 and 1964, the United States operated such a program—the Bracero Program—for agricultural labor from Mexico. Similar programs exist today in the United States to admit immigrants to work in agriculture for short periods without the right to reside permanently or become a U.S. citizen.

A second category of immigrant who has neither the rights and opportunities of the permanent resident, at least initially, nor the statutory exclusion of the undocumented is the **refugee** or **asylee**. Refugees are individuals who emigrate in the face of persecution in their home countries. Asylees are immigrants already present in the United States who cannot return to their home countries because they fear persecution upon return. As we will argue in Chapter 2, most countries find it very difficult to define what level of persecution merits these statuses. Political considerations in the receiving country often cloud the objective factors that should guide the award of refugee or asylee status.

Finally, almost all countries offer a form of short-term immigration for the purposes of tourism and commerce. Most tourists and businesspeople who travel internationally are not intent on staying in the receiving country and, hence, do not meet our definition of "immigrants," but some intending immigrants use the opportunity to get a short-term visitor or business visa as a ruse to enter a country and then stay on illegally. Although it might seem like modern, technologically adept countries like the United States should be able to control these visa overstayers, the difficulty in doing so is suggested by the fact that in 1993 (the last year for which we have comprehensive data), more than 23 million foreign nationals entered the United States as short-term visitors.

Each of these three possible routes to immigration other than permanent residence or undocumented immigration shares two characteristics: They do not offer immigrants the opportunity to attain a permanent status in the receiving country, and they offer some period during which they may live legally in the receiving country and assess opportunities to stay and, perhaps, seek to change their status to something more permanent. Thus, although these short-term or conditional statuses do not offer the opportunities of permanent residence or the risks of undocumented immigration, they do expand the pool of potential immigrants in the receiving society.

There is a final category of immigrant that meets part of our definition: people who move internationally. These are people who were forcibly moved from their homes to new nations for labor-related purposes. Specifically, these are people sold into slavery and transported abroad. We refer to slaves in our discussions as **involuntary immigrants**. As we will suggest, it is important to recognize that they are part of the immigrant flow during the period of their transport. In the United States, for example, the import of slaves reduced the demand for voluntary immigrants. As soon as the importation of slaves stopped, demand for voluntary immigrants surged. Equally important, over time the nation faced the same sort of questions concerning the freed slaves that it had with the incorporation of immigrants and their children into the political system. Although African immigrants in the period before 1820 had no choice in their migration, they did move from abroad and required legislative action and community organization to assure their eventual membership in the polity. Since 1820, the United States has officially eliminated involuntary immigration. However, it remains a form of international migration.

The diversity of legal statuses held by immigrants obscures one fundamental division—between those immigrants who have the right to become citizens of the receiving country and those who do not. **Naturalization** requirements vary from country to country. In the United States, immigrants to permanent residence may apply for naturalization after five years of legal residence. In addition to the five years of residence, the United States requires that naturalizing citizens complete

ILLUSTRATION 1.2   A Certificate of Naturalization

an application and demonstrate a knowledge of U.S. history and civics and of spoken, written, and oral English. Finally, and perhaps most important, the United States requires that the naturalizing citizen swear (or affirm) loyalty to the U.S. Constitution (see Illustration 1.2).

In this book, we highlight the dilemmas faced by the United States as a result of its continuing decisions to offer the opportunity to many to immigrate and to seek to incorporate those whom it admits to full membership in the polity. Throughout this discussion, it is important to keep in mind this simplified outline of the transition from migrant to naturalized citizen that we have provided here. The complexity of the legal barriers and personal and familial change that accompanies the move from one nation to another assures that for each immigrant, there are many detours and false starts that alter the outline. Nevertheless, the basic pattern remains. We should also note that the path is not unidirectional. Many immigrants never attain permanent resident status. Others become permanent residents but never naturalize. Some of these return to the home countries, others emigrate to third countries, and still others die as **denizens** in the United States.

Dilemmas: Immigration and Immigrants in the Contemporary United States

This book examines the choices that the United States faces in terms of immigration and immigrant **settlement** (the process of immigrant adaptation in the receiving country). Simply, we look at whom the United States allows to immigrate, what opportunities it offers these immigrants to become full members of the society as citizens once they have arrived, and how it structures the interaction between immigrants and U.S.-born populations. These topics are examined in Chapters 2, 3, and 4, respectively.

No one of these dilemmas is without controversy, and each entails short-term and long-term costs to the society. Over time, policymakers have concluded that these costs are more than compensated for by the contributions that immigrants make to U.S. society. These conclusions drawn in the past, however, will be continually reevaluated by each new generation. In this book we highlight these continuing dilemmas and indicate that none can be resolved as long as the United States continues to be a large-scale immigrant-receiving country and to offer these immigrants the opportunity for full membership as citizens.

In Chapter 2, we examine the continuing dilemma associated with immigration policy: How many immigrants should the nation admit, and what characteristics should they have? Over the nation's 210-year history, this dilemma has vexed policymakers and citizens alike and continues to do so in today's political and policy debates. Although there continue to be dissenting opinions, the nation since 1965 has embarked on a policy of large-scale immigration that primarily allocates access to two categories of immigrants: (1) immediate family members of U.S. citizens and permanent residents, and (2) immigrants with occupational skills that are needed in the U.S. economy. At this writing, however, this policy is being challenged by many who seek a reduction in the number of immigrants admitted to permanent residence.

In Chapter 3, we assess the dilemmas associated with the opportunities for membership offered to these immigrants once they arrive in the United States. The fundamental naturalization dilemma is this: Which immigrants should be incorporated, and on what terms? Although the naturalization issue is somewhat less controversial today than the immigration dilemma of how many immigrants to admit and what characteristics immigrants should have, naturalization is fundamental to the political health of the polity. Large-scale immigration without commensurate opportunities for incorporation would undermine the nation's democratic ideals. Blind admission of all immigrants to full membership without evaluating their interest in or attachment to American values and ideals would be equally disastrous. Thus, naturalization offers the state the opportunity to decide who should be incorporated and on what terms.

The dilemma outlined in Chapter 4 also grows from the decision to admit large numbers of immigrants to the United States. The state is increasingly faced with the question of how it structures the relationship between immigrants and the U.S.-born. This dilemma, unlike those discussed in Chapters 2 and 3, is more recent in origin, finding its roots primarily in the twentieth century. The steady expansion of the regulatory and social welfare functions of the state has increased its responsibilities in shaping interactions among individuals and groups. In the process, it has had to evaluate what rights and privileges to extend to noncitizens.

The state has also faced increasing demands to organize its various programs to provide for the settlement of immigrants. These efforts to assist immigrants sometimes come into conflict with the needs of the U.S.-born. Thus, the dilemma that we examine in Chapter 4 is this: How does the state shape the relationship between immigrants and natives?

As we will indicate, one final, overarching dilemma interacts with these three dilemmas about immigration, naturalization, and immigrant-native relations and it is therefore discussed throughout: What level of government should make and implement immigration, naturalization, and settlement policy? As we will indicate, national policy toward immigration and settlement has often conflicted with the interests of state and local governments. During the first century of the nation's history, the federal government took little role in setting policy toward immigration and immigrants. Into this vacuum, state and local governments set most policy in these areas. Beginning in this century, the federal government increased its involvement in both of these areas and sought to centralize its control. As we will show, the federal government has only met with mixed success in these efforts. In each chapter, then, we examine the question of federalism, or what level of government is empowered to make and implement policy in these areas.

2

Defining Who We Will Be: U.S. Immigration Policy

T HROUGHOUT U.S. HISTORY, citizens and leaders have accepted, praised, and revered immigrants. The symbolic notion of a "nation of immigrants" is richly entwined in the mythology of the United States. Intermittently, however, the public has also reacted against immigration and immigrants. Indeed, each of the major periods of welcome and acceptance has been shattered by popular reactions against immigration. Among the most famous reflections of these periods of anti-immigrant sentiment are the Alien and Sedition Acts, the American Know-Nothing Party, and the Red Scares at the end of World War I. The beginnings of another such popular reaction may be appearing as we write this book.

Despite these cycles of long-term acceptance of immigration and periodic anti-immigration fervor, the reverence for immigrants has remained strong. To the extent that it can be defined, this national proimmigrant ideology includes a notion that the United States is a nation of immigrants and that the nation's success is built on the labor and dreams of immigrants (see Illustration 2.1). In this chapter, we examine this seeming contradiction between love of immigrants and periodic opposition to immigration.

This contradiction sets the stage for the major ongoing dilemma in the creation of immigration policy, that is, the twin questions of how many immigrants the nation should admit and what characteristics they should have. For the first half of the nation's history, these questions were not asked, at least by policymakers. Increasingly, however, answering them has become a crucial dilemma for the polity. It is not an understatement to say that the answers to these questions—assuming that the United States continues to admit immigrants—will shape the future of the nation.

Once government establishes restrictions on immigration, it must decide who should enforce the restrictions and what should be done with people who migrate in violation of restrictions. Although seemingly simple, this is actually a complex question of the implementation of policy. It is simultaneously a question of federalism, that is, what level of government sets and enforces policy, and a question of balance, the issue of how immigration policy connects to other government objectives and activities. As we will suggest, immigration policy comes into conflict with domestic policies, particularly those concerning labor, as well as foreign policy.

Doonesbury   BY GARRY TRUDEAU

ILLUSTRATION 2.1   Doonesbury on Being American. *Doonesbury* © 1996, 1997 G. B. Trudeau. Reprinted with permission of *Universal Press Syndicate*. All rights reserved.

Broadly, then, this chapter focuses on the dilemma of deciding who we will be. First, we look at the ebbs and flows of immigration to the United States and the way the nation has restricted access to its borders. Second, we examine what level of government makes and enforces immigration policy and what happens when immigrants violate the immigration law; we also examine what happens when immigration policy comes into conflict with other domestic and foreign policies. Finally, we examine the contemporary debates over how many immigrants the United States should admit and what characteristics they should have. As we will show, this final issue is not unique to the contemporary era. Throughout U.S. history, Congress and the people have continually revisited the central dilemma of immigration policy—how many immigrants the nation should admit and what characteristics they should have.

Ebbs and Flows of Immigration to the United States

As Oscar Handlin noted, the history of America is the history of the immigrant (1951:3), and as he would have predicted, the story of American immigration in many ways presents an overview of the major phases of American history.

In this section, we review the history of immigration to the United States, dividing the discussion of immigration into four eras. The first era covers the country's earliest experiences with immigration and immigrants, events that in some cases occurred before the founding of the country. These early experiences shaped the way the Constitution approached immigration and settlement policy. The second era includes the first of the great waves of immigration to the United States, in the period between 1841 and 1860, when populations perceived of as different than the dominant populations entered the country in large numbers. In this first great wave of immigration, more than 1 million Irish and Germans entered the United States. The third phase begins with the end of the Civil War and continues to World War I. The final era, which extends to the present time, began formally in 1965, though its true inception was somewhat earlier.

For each of these four eras of immigration history, we examine who was immigrating and in what numbers, where these immigrants settled in the United States, their similarities and differences from previous immigrants and from the U.S.-born population, what economic and social opportunities were open to these immigrants, and, finally, how the United States reacted to large-scale immigration. It is this last aspect of our discussion that highlights the continuing dilemma in U.S. immigration policy. Each of these periods has witnessed high, and increasing, numbers of immigrants, yet each era concludes with a reaction against large-scale immigration. Further, in each of these periods, there was more restriction on immigration and selectivity of immigrants than during the preceding era.

This periodization of American immigration history necessarily clouds the bigger picture. To begin with, we can summarize the experience by saying that immigration has contributed a significant share of national population growth in the United States. It steadily increased from 1820, when governmental efforts to collect immigration data began, until 1920. Early in this period, Northwestern Europeans dominated the flow. By the period's end, Southern and Eastern Europeans had become most common among U.S. immigrants. The years from the 1920s through the 1950s saw a much lower level of immigration than the preceding decades. The 1930s, for example, witnessed the lowest levels of immigration since the 1830s. Although Europeans continued to be the most frequent immigrants, Mexicans for the first time were among the nationalities sending the most emigrants to the United States. Beginning in the 1960s, particularly after 1965 and continuing until today, the absolute level of immigration has returned to the levels seen around the turn of the century. The composition of this immigration has, however, changed markedly. Mexico, Latin America in general, and the Philippines, China, Korea, and Asia are the sources of the majority of immigrants to the United States. Tables 2.1 and 2.2 offer an overview of the number of immigrants and the four largest immigrant-sending countries by decade from the 1820s to 1996. Table 2.1 also indicates the share that immigrants from each decade added to the population at the beginning of the next decade.

Colonization of the New World and Immigration in the Revolutionary Era

It is a truism that all Americans, with the exception of Native Americans, trace their ancestry to immigrants. Even the Native American has migrant forebears in

TABLE 2.1 Immigration to the United States by Decade, 1820s–1990s, and Share of National Population Made Up of Previous Decade's Immigration

Decade	Number of Immigrants	Previous Decade's Immigration as a Percentage of National Population at Beginning of Next Decade
1821–1830	143,439	1.1%
1831–1840	599,125	3.5%
1841–1850	1,713,251	7.4%
1851–1860	2,598,214	8.3%
1861–1870	2,314,824[a]	5.8%
1871–1880	2,812,191	5.6%
1881–1890	5,246,613	8.3%
1891–1900	3,687,564	4.9%
1901–1910	8,795,386	9.6%
1911–1920	5,735,811	5.4%
1921–1930	4,107,209	3.3%
1931–1940	528,431	0.6%
1941–1950	1,035,039	0.7%
1951–1960	2,515,479	1.4%
1961–1970	3,321,677	1.6%
1971–1980	4,493,314	2.0%
1981–1990	7,328,062[b]	2.9%
1991–1996	6,146,213[b c]	NA

[a]Until 1867, the federal government recorded as immigrants only people who arrived at seaports.

[b]These figures include recipients of legalization under Immigration Reform and Control Act of 1986 who immigrated to the United States prior to 1982 but are recorded as having entered in year in which they received permanent residence.

[c]If the number of "new" immigrants for these six years holds constant throughout the decade, approximately 7.7 million immigrants will immigrate to permanent residence in the 1990s.

Sources: U.S. Bureau of the Census, 1993a, table 1; U.S. Immigration and Naturalization Service, 1992, table 8; U.S. Immigration and Naturalization Service, 1993, tables 1 and 9; U.S. Immigration and Naturalization Service, 1997; and Immigration and Naturalization Service web sites.

TABLE 2.2 Four Largest Immigrant Nationalities by Decade, 1820s–1980s

Decade and Country	Number of Immigrants	Percent of Decade's Immigration
1820s	143,439	–
Ireland	50,424	35.2
United Kingdom	25,079	17.5
France	8,497	5.9
Germany	6,761	4.7
1830s	599,125	–
Ireland	207,381	34.6
Germany	152,484	25.5
United Kingdom	75,810	12.7
France	45,575	7.6
1840s	1,713,251	–
Ireland	780,219	45.5
Germany	434,626	24.4
United Kingdom	267,044	15.6
France	77,262	4.5
1850s	2,598,214	–
Germany	951,667	36.6
Ireland	914,119	35.2
United Kingdom	423,974	16.3
France	76,358	2.9
1860s	2,314,824	–
Germany	787,468	34.0
United Kingdom	606,896	26.2
Ireland	435,778	18.8
Canada and Newfoundland	153,878	6.6
1870s	2,812,191	–
Germany	718,182	25.8
United Kingdom	548,043	19.5
Ireland	436,871	15.5
Canada and Newfoundland	383,640	13.6
1880s	5,246,613	–
Germany	1,452,970	27.7
United Kingdom	807,357	15.4
Ireland	655,482	12.5
Norway-Sweden	568,362	10.8

(continues)

TABLE 2.2 *(continued)*

Decade and Country	Number of Immigrants	Percent of Decade's Immigration
1890s	3,687,564	–
Italy	651,893	17.7
Austria-Hungary	592,707	16.1
Soviet Union[a]	505,290	13.7
Germany	505,152	13.7
1900s	8,765,386	–
Austria-Hungary	2,145,266	24.5
Italy	2,045,877	23.3
Soviet Union[a]	1,597,306	18.2
United Kingdom	525,950	6.0
1910s	5,735,811	–
Italy	1,109,524	19.3
Soviet Union[a]	921,201	16.1
Austria-Hungary	896,342	15.6
Canada and Newfoundland	742,185	12.9
1920s	4,107,209	–
Canada and Newfoundland	924,515	22.5
Mexico	459,287	11.2
Italy	455,315	11.1
Germany	412,202	10.0
1930s	528,431	–
Germany	114,058	21.6
Canada and Newfoundland	108,527	20.5
Italy	68,028	12.9
United Kingdom	31,572	6.0
1940s	1,035,039	–
Germany	226,578	21.9
Canada and Newfoundland	171,718	16.6
United Kingdom	139,306	13.5
Mexico	60,569	5.9
1950s	2,515,479	–
Germany	477,765	19.0
Canada and Newfoundland	377,952	15.0
Mexico	299,811	11.9
United Kingdom	202,824	8.1

(continues)

TABLE 2.2 *(continued)*

Decade and Country	Number of Immigrants	Percent of Decade's Immigration
1960s	3,321,677	–
Mexico	453,937	13.7
Canada and Newfoundland	413,310	12.4
Italy	214,111	6.4
United Kingdom	213,822	6.4
1970s	4,493,314	–
Mexico	640,294	14.2
Philippines	354,987	7.9
Korea	267,638	6.0
Cuba	264,863	5.9
1980s	7,328,062[b]	–
Mexico	1,655,843[b]	14.0
Philippines	548,764[b]	4.6
China	346,747[b]	2.9
Korea	333,746[b]	2.8

[a]The Immigration and Naturalization Service categorizes Russia as the Soviet Union prior to 1917. Prior to 1919, the Soviet Union category includes immigrants from parts of today's Poland.

[b]These figures include recipients of legalization under Immigration Reform and Control Act of 1986 who immigrated to the United States prior to 1982 but are recorded as having entered in year in which they received permanent residence.

Source: U.S. Immigration and Naturalization Service, 1993, tables 1 and 2.

Asia. The arrivals of the earliest European and African immigrants are relatively well documented. The historical record notes the arrival of the Spanish missionaries at St. Augustine in 1565, the Spanish settlement of the New Mexico colony in 1598, the founding of Jamestown in 1607, and the arrival of the first slave in Virginia in 1619. Thus, the arrival of the Pilgrims in Massachusetts in 1620, though celebrated as being the national symbol of early immigration, was in reality late in the period of initial European colonization of territory that later became the United States.

By the 1630s, however, immigration to what was to become the United States was so common that individual arrivals and even the total number of immigrants went unrecorded. This was so for nearly two centuries, during which immigration to the colonies and then to the new United States was largely unregulated by these receiving governments. Immigration during this first phase of American immigrant history differs somewhat from the periods that followed, yet patterns developed in this period that were to repeat themselves throughout U.S. history.

Prerevolutionary Immigration, 1630–1776. Approximately 600,000 immigrants moved to North America in the seventeenth century. The majority of them settled outside of the territory that would become the United States. The best available estimates indicate that between 1630 and 1700, approximately 155,000 English immigrated to the British colonies (Altman and Horn 1991:4). These English immigrants accounted for approximately 90 percent of European immigrants to the colonies. The next-largest group of future Americans, the African slaves who began to populate the Southern plantations, were forced into their status. As we indicated in Chapter 1, we refer to African slaves as "involuntary immigrants." Although they did not enter the immigrant stream voluntarily, the slaves, once freed after the Civil War, presented incorporation dilemmas for the polity like those of the voluntary immigrants. Further, their forced immigration reduced the demand for the labor of voluntary migrants from Europe.

Immigration levels increased vastly in the eighteenth century. During a rare period of no European wars between 1713 and 1765, approximately 350,000 Europeans and Africans settled in the British colonies in North America. Approximately 40 percent of these prerevolutionary eighteenth-century immigrants were involuntary immigrants—Africans destined for slavery. The Europeans who immigrated in this period were much more diverse in origin than those of the previous century. They included approximately 100,000 Irish, who themselves included the descendants of Scottish Presbyterians who had migrated to Ireland in the sixteenth century. The Germans, the next-largest nationality among the prerevolutionary immigrants, numbered approximately 65,000. Also included in the immigrant stream to the British colonies in this period were Dutch and Scottish immigrants. Despite the surge in immigration in the period leading to the American Revolution, the engine of population growth in the colonies was as much high fertility rates and increasing life expectancy as immigration. Of the 3.9 million people counted in the first census, only a small percentage of them had been born outside the colonies.

These groups by no means make up the full range of immigrants to territories that were to become the United States. Spanish colonies in Florida and the Southwest and French colonies in the Louisiana Territory thrived in this period. These settlements, however, never developed the density of population that the British colonies did. Instead, both France and Spain established vast territorial claims based on networks of fortified trading posts and missions. By 1720, these networks covered two-thirds of what is today the continental United States. Still, there was little to attract immigrants to these areas, so the European- and African-origin population, whether foreign-born or Americas-born, never exceeded 50,000.

In addition to nationality, the major distinction among European immigrants to the British colonies before the Revolution related to the way in which they were able to afford passage to the colonies. Some were able to immigrate based on their own or family resources. These included governmental officials, clergy, merchants, artisans, farmers, gentry, and lesser nobility seeking to make their way in the New World. Generally, these immigrants had skills, or capital, or worked in one of a narrow set of professions.

The mass of immigrants, however, came as **indentured laborers** or convicts. The indentured servants were required to perform between two and eight years of labor to repay the price of their passage. The convicts faced different requirements, based both on their sentences and on the types and location of their labor in the colonies. For the most part, the indentured servants and convicts had no capital and few skills, other than their ability to perform arduous labor. The lack of capital forced many of the seventeenth-century indentured servants to continue to work beyond the term of their original contract because of the lack of greater opportunities. As land in the West became available and safe from raids by Native Americans, however, indentured servants (both those under contract and those who had fulfilled their contractual responsibilities) began to discover other opportunities. These opportunities for European immigrants in the expanding frontier and the high number who fled their contracts steadily reduced the appeal of indentured servants to many landholders. In their place, African slaves steadily came to be used in greater numbers.

Although indentured servitude declined as a source of new immigrants, it represents an early form of **labor recruitment** as an incentive to immigration. The explicit trade of passage to the United States for a specific period of service in indentured servitude became more muddied after its decline, but labor recruitment continued to be an important source of immigrants to the United States well into the twentieth century. When the Congress began to explore ways to limit immigration in the nineteenth century, one of its early targets was immigrants who had been recruited abroad for jobs in specific industries or regions in the United States.

Immigrants of different legal statuses and nationalities did not spread evenly across the colonies. The immigration patterns of indentured servants and then the slaves, for example, were focused on the middle colonies and the South, respectively. Most New England residents were free and of English or Welsh origin. Generally, as the immigration patterns we have discussed would suggest, the English and Welsh were found throughout the colonies. These English and Welsh immigrants did not, however, dominate throughout the colonies. New York City and the Hudson Valley had large Dutch populations. German immigrants dominated the flow to Philadelphia and eastern Pennsylvania. Convicts were most likely to end up in the Chesapeake Bay region. Finally, the South saw concentrations of Africans, Germans, Scots, and Scots-Irish.

Each of these immigrant populations found a home in the New World, but initially each sought to create cultural links to the world they left behind. In terms of language, each population retained the home tongue. The Germans, in particular, sought to maintain their mother tongue by establishing German language schools. These early immigrants also maintained a bond with their roots through religion. In this case, the link was more localized than the linguistic tie. Many of the early colonists were religious minorities in their home countries that sought a greater religious freedom in their adopted home. Tolerance varied from colony to colony, but the effect was to create a religious mosaic throughout the territories, which eventually necessitated the constitutional guarantee of religious freedom.

The large-scale immigration to the colonies was not without conflict. Mirroring debates held throughout U.S. immigration history, the Pennsylvania legislature passed a tax on foreigners entering the territory. Though quickly repealed, this tax sought to undermine the efforts by the territorial governor to promote immigration, particularly of Germans. In this debate, the governor saw the economic advantage of new settlers, whereas the legislature represented mass concerns about cultural change and economic competition (Muller 1992:18–19). In several other colonies, anti-Catholic sentiments shaped people's thinking about immigration. Interestingly, this religious bigotry, though pervasive, did not result in successful efforts to prevent Catholic immigration. Instead, it manifested itself in efforts to limit the civil rights of Catholics.

Thus, despite some objections to specific groups of immigrants and their unequal treatment upon arrival, the British colonies actively sought new immigrants. The availability of land and the need for labor reduced the popular opposition to immigration. Moreover, a slow shift in British policy away from promoting immigration to the colonies in the years leading up to the Revolution contributed to the colonial sentiment that separation from Britain was necessary. The popular desire for continued immigration appears in the Declaration of Independence. One of the charges against King George III was that "he has endeavored to prevent the population of these states . . . refusing to pass others to encourage their migration hither."

The patterns of immigration and native reaction to immigration and immigrants that appeared in this prerevolutionary period have repeated themselves through U.S. history. Immigrants did not settle evenly throughout the colonies. In the places where they did and particularly in places where the new immigrants differed culturally or religiously from the U.S.-born, cultural conflicts led to localized efforts to restrict immigration. It should be noted the prerevolutionary opposition to immigration focused primarily on cultural dimensions of the relations between immigrants and natives.

Immigration to the New United States, 1787–1840. The Revolution slowed immigration to the United States, and the defeat of the British spurred an emigration among British loyalists. With the end of the war, however, immigration soon resumed, and the number of immigrants rapidly grew.

Although the Constitution does not address the issue of immigration, a quick review of the opinions of key national leaders demonstrates that there was a consensus, at least at the elite level, supporting unlimited immigration of white Europeans. George Washington spoke of the new United States as welcoming not only the "opulent and respected stranger" but also "the oppressed and persecuted of all Nations and Religions" (quoted in Muller 1992:19). Thomas Jefferson expressed some fears about the political assimilation of immigrants from nations ruled by absolute monarchs, but he also advocated government policies to attract immigrants who were wealthy or skilled. Further, Jefferson anticipated a problem that was to plague immigration in future years. He was concerned that if immigrants were to concentrate in one region, they would maintain their language and customs and be slower to assimilate, but this concern did not temper his support for an open immigration policy for Europeans. In sum, the leaders of the new United States welcomed immigrants from Europe.

The Constitution was more explicit concerning the forced immigration of Africans to slavery. Although they worded the statement ambiguously in the document, the framers of the Constitution prohibited Congress from restricting the importation of slaves prior to 1808 (Article 1, Section 9). The Constitution granted Congress the power to levy a head tax of up to $10 per slave, a considerable sum in that era.

During the nation's early years, there were few laws concerning immigration, and most that were enacted until the Civil War addressed transatlantic shipping and reporting requirements for the ships bringing immigrants to the United States. We summarize major federal legislation concerning immigration in Table 2.3.

During the first decade of the country's history, this elite consensus supporting unfettered European immigration gave way to a period of anti-immigrant fervor that reached its peak with the passage of the **Alien and Sedition Acts** (1798). The origins of these concerns were domestic and international. Domestically, the party then in control—the Federalist Party—saw the immigrants as a potential source of support for their emerging opposition—the Jeffersonians, or Demo-

TABLE 2.3 Summary of Major Federal Immigration Laws, 1787–1997

1787–1875	*Minimal Federal Regulation Focusing Primarily on Transportation of Immigrants*
Year	*Major Provisions of Legislation*
1798	Deportation of aliens dangerous to the United States and reporting requirements for captains of passenger vessels.
1819	Ship captains must deliver passenger lists to customs officials (immigration data begin with the implementation of this law).
1847	"Passenger Acts"—legislation to protect passengers, including immigrants, on passenger vessels.
1855	Required ship captains to provide separate reporting of immigrants arriving for permanent residence and immigrants arriving for temporary residence.
1862	Prohibited transportation of Chinese "coolies" on American vessels.
1864	Created a Commissioner of Immigration in the State Department and permitted labor contracting in which the immigrant exchanged future labor for the cost of transportation.

1875–1965	**Immigration Restriction and National-Origin Quotas**
Year	*Major Provisions of Legislation*
1875	Prohibited the immigration of criminals, prostitutes, and "Orientals" who did not freely and voluntarily consent to immigration.
1882	Suspended the immigration of Chinese laborers for 10 years (subsequently extended until 1943) and added to the restricted categories for non-Chinese immigrants to exclude persons likely to become a public charge.
1885	"Contract Labor Law"—prohibited immigrants who had contracted to perform specific services (exceptions were made for temporary immigrants).
1891	Bureau of Immigration established in the Treasury Department; prohibited immigration of persons suffering from contagious diseases, felons, polygamists, and aliens whose passage was paid by others; empowered Secretary of Treasury to establish rules for inspection along U.S. land borders; and directed deportation for immigrants who entered the United States in violation of U.S. law.
1903	Prohibited the immigration of anarchists and mandated deportation of immigrants who became public charges within two years of immigration.
1907	Prohibited immigration of imbeciles, feebleminded persons, persons with physical or mental defects, children unaccompanied by their parents, and women coming to the United States for immoral purposes.
1917	Prohibited the immigration of the illiterate and created the "barred zone" that excluded all Asians from immigration.

(continues)

TABLE 2.3 *(continued)*

Year	Major Provisions of Legislation
1921	First "National Origin Quota" law—established cap of 350,000 immigrants annually and allocated immigration visas based on the number of foreign-born persons of each nationality in the 1910 census; exempted the Western Hemisphere from these restrictions.
1924	Second "National Origin Quota" law—set annual quota at 164,667 and allocated visas based on the 1890 census (later changed to 150,000 and the 1920 census); established preference quota system to facilitate the immigration of immediate family members of U.S. citizens and residents; and established consular control system to issue visas abroad.
1929	Registry established to legalize undocumented immigrants resident for eight years.
1937	Mandated deportation of immigrants who secured a visa by fraud through contracting marriage to a U.S. citizen.
1940	Mandated registration of all immigrants in the United States.
1943	Established "Bracero Program" to provide short-term agricultural labor and made Chinese eligible for immigration (their initial quota was 105 annually).
1945	Waived visa requirements for "war brides."
1948	First refugee law—provided for immigration of up to 205,000 persons displaced by World War II.
1950	Prohibited immigration of current and former members of the Communist Party, the Nazi Party, and other totalitarian organizations.
1952	Criminalized facilitating undocumented immigration or harboring undocumented immigrants (employing an undocumented immigrant not classified as harboring); expanded powers of the Border Patrol to investigate undocumented immigration; amended national-origin quotas to base the quota on the 1920 census and all persons of each national ancestry or origin with each Asian country awarded no more than 2,000 visas.
1957	Modified refugee admissions so that a surge in one year would not have to be mortgaged against immigration from that country in future years.
1961	Eliminated ceiling of 2,000 visas from Asian countries.
1964	Terminated Bracero Program.

*1965–1997   Family Preferences, Controlling Refugee/Asylee Admissions,
and Controlling Undocumented Immigrations*

Year	Major Provisions of Legislation
1965	Abolished national-origin quota system and replaced it with a first-come, first-served system rewarding potential immigrants with immediate family in the United States and with special or needed job skills; established

(continues)

TABLE 2.3   *(continued)*

Year	Major Provisions of Legislation
	per-country limit of 20,000 immigrants (immediate family members did not count against this limit); exempted Western Hemisphere from per-country limit, but established regional limit of 120,000.
1976	Applied 20,000 per-country limit to the Western Hemisphere.
1980	First comprehensive legislation to address refugee admissions—eliminated refugees as a category in the preference system.
1981	Further expanded INS powers to combat undocumented immigration, including the ability to seize property used to facilitate undocumented immigration.
1986	Immigration Reform and Control Act of 1986—authorized "legalization" for undocumented immigrants who had resided in the United States since before January 1, 1982, and agricultural workers with shorter residences; created sanctions for employers knowingly hiring undocumented immigrants and established requirement to prove work eligibility before starting a job; increased enforcement at the borders; and provided for new agricultural labor immigration during periods of agricultural labor shortage.
1986	Established two-year "conditional" permanent residence for aliens deriving their immigrant status through marriage to a U.S. citizen (to control marriage fraud).
1990	Increased total preference immigration to a flexible cap of 675,000 and expanded border enforcement and grounds for deportation.
1996	Expanded and speeded removal process for undocumented immigrants and asylum applicants denied asylee status; made immigrant sponsorship legally enforceable and raised the financial level necessary to sponsor an immigrant; terminated permanent resident eligibility for most federal social welfare programs (both for immigrants already resident in the United States and for those who would immigrate after the law was enacted); and reduced judicial oversight of asylum and deportation proceedings.
1997	Supplemental Security Income program eligibility restored for permanent resident immigrants.

cratic Republicans. Internationally, the cause was the French Revolution and the political turbulence that it spurred throughout Europe. Political refugees from the European tumult arrived in the United States. Many in the United States feared that the ideas of these political refugees—on all sides of the ideological spectrum—would destabilize the new U.S. democracy. Interestingly, Congress tried to control not immigration but naturalization in this era. This concern about immigrants ended rapidly with the election of Thomas Jefferson in 1800, which led to the repeal of the acts.

Although there are no exact numbers, voluntary immigration in the period between the end of the Revolution and the 1820s slowed from prerevolutionary levels and probably did not exceed 2,000 people per year. In part, this decline resulted from British efforts to restrict emigration (which lasted until the 1820s). Also, the wars that raged through Europe in this period increased the difficulties of securing transport.

The composition of the postrevolutionary voluntary immigration was not significantly changed from the prerevolutionary period. British and Scottish immigrants dominated the flow in these decades. Most of these British and Scottish immigrants settled in the cities of the Northeast.

Like their prerevolutionary predecessors, these immigrants experienced considerable economic opportunity. A major reason for this is that although the number of immigrants rose and declined with the cyclical nature of the U.S. economy, immigrants of this era, like most in the early nineteenth century, had the option of domestic migration westward. This geographic mobility—both of immigrants and U.S.-born populations—reduced the potential for the formation of cohesive ethnic communities and also reduced the likelihood of anti-immigrant movements by the U.S.-born in the cities and regions where the immigrants first settled.

The First Great Wave, 1840–1860

The slow but steady flow of immigrants that characterized the postrevolutionary period became a torrent in the 1840s and 1850s. Whereas annual immigration levels had numbered approximately 14,000 in the 1820s and 60,000 in the 1830s, the pace quickened to 171,000 yearly in the 1840s and rose to 260,000 yearly in the 1850s (U.S. Immigration and Naturalization Service 1993). The 2.6 million immigrants who arrived in the United States during the 1850s composed 8.3 percent of the national population counted in the 1860 census.

Higher numbers were not the only change in this period. The national origin of the immigrants in the First Great Wave differed significantly from the immigrants who had come before. In the 1820s, Germans and Irish made up just four in ten immigrants. By the 1840s and 1850s, this proportion increased to seven in ten. In addition to the new national origins of the majority of immigrants, the Germans and Irish introduced a second element of diversity—religion. The majority of the Irish immigrants were Roman Catholic; many of the German immigrants were Jewish. Before this era, most immigrants and natives had been Protestants.

As is frequently the case with immigrants, the Germans, Irish, and others who arrived in the 1840s and 1850s did not spread themselves evenly across the country. Instead, they concentrated in Northeastern cities. Germans moved to New York, Philadelphia, and Boston. Fully 90 percent of the Irish immigrants in this period also immigrated to Northeastern cities, again particularly New York, Philadelphia, and Boston (Seller 1988:71).

These immigrants joined a migration of U.S.-born Americans from rural areas to the cities, which stimulated substantial growth in urban areas. Between 1800 and 1860, the share of the U.S. population in urban areas grew from 6 to nearly 20 percent, with New York City as perhaps the most extreme example of this growth. It grew from a town of 60,000 in 1800 into a city of 1 million by 1860 (Seller 1988:72).

The growth of the cities and the increasing volume of immigrants created a new dynamic in the history of immigration. Immigrants began to concentrate in the cities, and the character of cities came to overlap with immigrant ethnic populations. Thus, the concentration of the Irish and German immigrants (particularly German Jewish immigrants) in the cities of the Northeast, particularly in New York, shaped the future economic and social options of these populations and shaped the national perceptions of those cities. After this period, discussions of the "problems" of cities were often veiled ethnic references to immigrants and their descendants.

The social impact of this influx went beyond simply increasing the national population and the relative size of the urban population. These immigrants challenged the dominant culture of the United States. This challenge had two aspects—language and religion. The German immigrants of this era spoke a language other than English, whereas previous immigrants had been English speakers. Perhaps of greater consequence was religion. As previously noted, the overwhelming majority of Irish immigrants were Roman Catholic and many of the German immigrants were Jewish. Although most immigrants of this era learned English, few non-Protestant immigrants converted to Protestant faiths.

Despite these differences, the country absorbed ever increasing numbers of immigrants. To understand why, it is important to briefly consider what these immigrants brought with them. For the most part, they were unskilled, and their origins were rural. Although the economic opportunities available in the United States certainly guided the destination decision, privation and social change in the home countries acted as catalysts to emigration. The Irish fled the **Great Potato Famine,** which caused a million deaths between 1845 and 1851. Throughout Germany and Europe in general, this period was one of poor harvests and political unrest that spurred many to emigrate.

How could the United States absorb these immigrants, most of whom were unskilled? The needs of the economy in that era were different from those of today. The level of industrialization of the mid-nineteenth century required little more of labor than brawn and a willingness to work. This is not to say that the United States attracted only unskilled immigrants. Skilled European workers seeking to take advantage of the better wages and better opportunities in the United States also immigrated during this era. Even so, the vast majority of immigrants in the First Great Wave had few skills. The level to which they succeeded economically varied with the ups and downs of the economy. There were few social services, so survival depended on work and the charity of family members and friends. Thus, as we suggested in Chapter 1, immigration resulted from a combination of push factors, in this case food shortages, population growth, and political unrest in Europe, and pull factors, that is, demand for unskilled labor, the expansion and decline in cost of transatlantic shipping, and labor recruitment, which in combination spurred immigration to the United States.

By this point in U.S. immigration history, the average immigrant was for the most part poorer and less educated than the average U.S.-born citizen. This gap did not, however, cause as much conflict as it did for later generations of immigrants. First, the differences rapidly narrowed or disappeared, particularly for immigrants who left the Northeastern cities. In this era, the federal government distributed land in the West to homesteaders (people who lived on the land and promised to farm the land). The states and territories of the West sought population and included immigrants (and potential immigrants abroad) among the targeted populations. Second, the overwhelming majority of the U.S.-born population in this era resided in rural areas. Thus, the immigrants who stayed in the cities—as the majority did—did not challenge the economic well-being of the majority of the U.S.-born.

Cultural conflict did, however, appear. The **American, or "Know-Nothing," Party** emerged in the early 1850s with anti-immigrant mobilization as part of its platform. Central to its agenda was a concern about immigrants, particularly about the cultural and political differences that the Know-Nothings perceived came from immigration. One of the Know-Nothing demands was for an extension of the period prior to naturalization from five years to twenty-one years (more on this in the next chapter). The Know-Nothing Party reached its peak in the 1856 election, but it never strongly influenced national immigration policy. Its decline, however, was not necessarily a reflection of national support for immigration. Instead, the Civil War reshaped U.S. politics and the party system. Concern over immigration policy was lost in the bigger controversies of the day, and widespread opposition to immigration disappeared for nearly thirty years.

In sum, the Know-Nothings reflected concern among some U.S.-born Americans about immigration and immigrants. Overwhelmingly, though, immigrants in the First Great Wave were welcomed and immediately incorporated into the national economy. Through domestic migration, immigrants had access to an immediate social mobility that would not characterize later generations of immigrants. Even in this era, though, the culturally or religiously distinct immigrants (the Irish and the German Jews) were less likely to move beyond the cities.

The Second Great Wave, 1870–1920

The anti-immigrant fervor of the 1850s was lost to the greater national tumult of the Civil War (Anbinder 1992). Although the immediate impact of the Civil War was to slow immigration, the Northern victory began a period of steadily increasing immigration that was to last for fifty years. Although immigration expanded steadily throughout this period, it was also a period of increasing restriction. This wave of immigration ended with the most draconian restrictions that the United States has ever imposed. Thus, the Second Great Wave was a period of vast immigration as well as a time of increasing selection in who could immigrate and in what numbers.

Between 1870 and 1920, more than 26 million people immigrated to the United States. Immigrants in this period alone exceeded the national population in 1850. The symbolism of the immigration of this period is still with us today. The Statue of Liberty appeared in New York Harbor, and **Ellis Island** came into use as an immigration processing station in this era. It was also during this era that the national proimmigrant ideology was first articulated, in part to serve as a device to unify the nation during a period of unprecedented immigration.

The Second Great Wave is significant for three reasons. First, the immigrants of the Second Great Wave settled throughout the nation. Second, they began to come from Asia and the Americas as well as from Europe and Africa. Finally, this era saw the federal government assert control over the creation of immigration policy.

In the period just after the Civil War, immigrants resembled those who had come during the First Great Wave. In the 1860s, 1870s, and 1880s, Germany, the United Kingdom, and Ireland were the top three sending countries, accounting for over half of total immigration in each of these decades. Beginning in the late 1880s, the composition shifted considerably. Southern and Eastern Europeans replaced the Northern and Western Europeans. These "new" immigrants came from such countries as Italy, Austria-Hungary, and Russia (after 1917, the Soviet Union). Each of these countries had made up a relatively small share of immigrants prior to 1880 but collectively came to provide more than 40 percent of immigrants between 1890 and 1920.

A final trend to note in the composition of immigration of this era is that Canadians and Mexicans began to account for large numbers of immigrants. As early as the 1860s and again in the 1870s and 1910s, Canada sent the fourth-largest number of immigrants. In this same period, immigration across the southern border also increased. Immigration from Mexico does not rank in the top four sending countries until the 1920s, but this may be because the level to which Mexican immigration was recorded was sporadic until 1917 (Sánchez 1993). Thus, from 1865 to 1920, there was not only a vast increase in the number of immigrants coming to the United States each year but also a diversification in the origins of the immigrants, starting with Europe and then spreading to other parts of the world.

It was with the growing immigration of these "new" immigrants that anti-immigrant concerns began to rise again. In the popular imagination, the "new" immigrants came to be seen as less capable than their predecessors—less capable of working, less capable of learning American ways, and less capable of assimilating. As the concerns among the U.S.-born population about the new immigrants grew, restrictionist efforts became more active. Eventually, this concern about immigration generated the severe reductions in immigration of the 1920s—the **National Origin Restrictions** (or "**Quota Acts**")—that we will discuss later in this section.

The vast majority of the immigrants of the Second Great Wave, like their predecessors, moved to cities, particularly the cities of the East Coast and the industrial Midwest. The rapid growth in the cities of this era was driven in large part by rapid immigration. It is important to note that some nationalities—particularly Scandinavians, Germans, and Mexicans—migrated directly to rural areas.

Many of the immigrants moved almost immediately into industrial jobs. Recruitment to these positions often began in the sending countries and intensified when immigrants reached a U.S. port. Steamship companies conducted the initial stage of the labor recruitment, often using representatives in Europe. Often the steamship companies represented specific employers, industries, or regions of the United States seeking to expand their pool of immigrant labor. The cost of passage was often subsidized in order to attract needed labor. At the U.S. port, additional incentives were offered to immigrants to go to specific regions or even with specific employers. The intensified recruitment of immigrants in this era partially explains the changing national origins of immigrants.

States and cities also sought to attract immigrants. In the case of states, the recruiters included Midwestern states seeking to add to their populations. In the case of cities, recruitment focused on assuring a sufficient labor supply for new industries. Certainly, these patterns indicate that immigrants, or at least the labor of immigrants, were welcome in this era and, to some, were perceived to be in short supply.

The diversification of immigrant origins in this period reflects both changes in the sending countries—expansion of transportation infrastructure and disruption of traditional labor relationships—and also the ever expanding demand in the United States (as well as in other parts of the Americas, particularly Argentina and Brazil). Although emigration had been restricted formally and informally in earlier periods, the late nineteenth century saw virtually no restrictions by European states. On the contrary, many governments used emigration as a tool to maintain domestic tranquillity. Interestingly, in the late nineteenth century, the countries that sought to restrict emigration were those that would later send many nationals to the United States—Mexico and China. Mexico sought to keep peasants on the land, and China yielded to diplomatic pressure from the United States to exclude Chinese immigrants.

Throughout this period, it was more common for men to be in the immigrant stream than women. Many men immigrated without their wives or families, though far fewer women embarked on the journey without first having family in the United States. The technological advances of the shipping industry in this era, however, made it increasingly easy for immigrants to return to their countries of origin ("return migration") and for families to follow after one family member had established a beachhead in the United States. Thus, the sex ratio of immigrants increasingly approached 1:1.

Return migration was not new to this era. It was, however, possible at a previously unattainable scale. In the Spanish and French colonies of the New World, return migration was the most common pattern, particularly early in the colonial era. In the British colonies, by contrast, the vast majority of migrants did not return to Europe, nor did they plan to. Those who did were often the most elite migrants. Some of the nonelite immigrants in the British colonies and later in the United States did, of course, return to Europe, though their numbers were always small. In the 1740s, Benjamin Franklin observed this phenomenon and worried that what he called the "reverse flow" would counterbalance the new immigrants. Franklin's fears were unfounded then and have continued to be since. Even in the early twentieth century, when return migration became more affordable and less arduous (and when data on rates first became available), estimates indicate that no more than 35 percent of immigrants returned to their home countries (Wyman 1993). Return migration rates varied considerably among national-origin groups in this era. As many as 90 percent of Bulgarian, Serbian, and Montenegrin immigrants returned to Europe. For Northern Italians, the rate was just 11 percent. Although not from a single country, "Hebrews" had the lowest rates of return, at just 5 percent.

During the Second Great Wave, seasonal labor migration appeared for the first time among immigrants from Europe. Some immigrants in this era migrated several times over a series of years. Although many eventually stayed on permanently, others returned to their home countries in the end.

A family member's setting out to test the waters before others immigrated (or did not) was also not new to this era of U.S. immigration, but it became much more common. Earlier generations of immigrants had primarily come either with their families (the prerevolutionary immigrants and the more affluent or skilled in later periods) or without them (many of the convicts and the early Irish and German immigrants). In this post–Civil War era, the pattern of sequential migration that continues among immigrants today first appeared on a large scale. One family member would immigrate, earn money for others to migrate, and ease the transition for subsequent migrants.

The ease of family immigration and of return migration created conflicting pressures on the immigrant. With their families in the United States and their children raised here, immigrants could make their lives in the United States. This could lead to the development of social attachment and political loyalty to the United States. Whereas the potential for family immigration created an incentive to develop a permanent attachment to the United States, the ease of return migration offered an incentive to maintain ties to the sending country.

Clearly, these attachments—to the United States and to the home country—are not mutually exclusive. Immigrants in this era began a process that continues today. The process of becoming American is by no means immediate but rather occurs for many immigrants steadily over time. The presence of family in the United States speeds the process for many immigrants.

In the period after the Civil War, immigrants experienced a new incentive to develop an attachment to the United States. The cities to which most immigrated, at least initially, were under the control of **urban political machines**. In most cities, these machines were themselves controlled by **first- and second-generation immigrants**. In other words, they were controlled by the children of people who had immigrated in the early part of the nineteenth century or by people who themselves had immigrated to the United States after the Civil War. These machines served several important roles for immigrants. They provided a crude social welfare system, at least for the co-nationals and political supporters of machine leaders. The machine also provided jobs for some new arrivals and food or other emergency needs in times of crisis. As the national and state governments provided no such assistance, this machine-sponsored assistance was often crucial to immigrant survival. The machines also acted as intermediaries between immigrants and nonimmigrants. Crude as it was, the machine assistance was often the immigrants' first contact with American life. As we will show in the next chapter, the machines served a final role for some immigrants—assistance with naturalization and socialization to voting. It was these immigrant votes that allowed the machines to remain in power throughout the late nineteenth and early twentieth centuries (Erie 1988).

Machine outreach to recent immigrants aside, immigrant life in the cities of the Northeast and Midwest in this period was quite dismal. Housing conditions were poor; work opportunities were exploitative and often dangerous; and crime and disease were rife. Women and children worked in the factories, with no added protections and less pay than adult men. Formal education lasted no more than four years for most children. Nationalistic rivalries from Europe carried over to the New World and were often inflamed by political leaders seeking to control immigrant populations. Life for many immigrants involved few who were not co-nationals, even in the workforce, which tended to be segregated by national-origin group. Thus, many immigrants did not assimilate linguistically or geographically. Although opportunities for internal migration within the United States continued to exist, the availability of land in the West that had characterized the early years of the nineteenth century had disappeared. Thus, immigrants in the Second Great Wave, or at least those who immigrated to urban areas, did not experience the rapid upward social mobility or assimilation of the previous immigrants. More often than not, this upward social mobility and assimilation occurred not for the immigrants themselves but instead for their children or grandchildren.

Roots of Immigration Restriction.   With the exception of the prohibition on importing slaves, the United States had not barred immigrants from its shores during most of the nation's first century. Immigration had been taxed by local governments, but this policy was understood as a tool to generate revenues, not to restrict immigration. During the Second Great Wave, however, policymakers experimented with various restrictions. As we will suggest, these efforts increased dramatically between 1875 and the end of the Second Great Wave in the early 1920s. The end of this period saw the most draconian restrictions that the United States has ever placed on immigration. Equally important, the process of establishing immigration restrictions centralized control over immigration with the federal government and spurred an increased federal role in border enforcement.

We review the specific restrictions here in order to examine how the United States moved in fifty years from virtually unrestricted immigration to the most severe limits in the country's two-hundred-year history. Beyond the specific limitations discussed, it is important to note that the process of establishing limits was accompanied by a steady centralization of immigration administration. At the start of the period, limits were largely meaningless because the federal government did not have the capacity to control the actions of local government officials. By the end, to enter the country legally, immigrants had to have visas issued abroad before they could begin their journey, and federal employees were in place at ports of entry to assure that immigrants had the proper documentation. Thus, the immigration restrictionist effort that culminated in the Quota Acts of 1921 and 1924 shifted responsibility for immigration policymaking to the federal government.

In 1875, Congress placed the first restriction on immigration by individuals other than Africans destined for slavery. U.S. immigration law excluded criminals, prostitutes, and contract labor from Asia (18 *Statutes at Large* 477, enacted March 3, 1875). Spurred by competing impulses, Congress responded in this legislation to growing public concern about specific forms of immigration. At this point, there was no national or policymaker consensus against *all* immigration. Instead, in this early phase of anti-immigration efforts, Congress targeted specific classes of immigration. The government also developed administrative mechanisms, such as the placement of federal immigration personnel at major ports of entry and oversight of the steamship companies, to exclude these specific classes of immigrants.

Non-Asians in California sought to restrict the economic power of Chinese immigrants. Thus, Congress responded to concerns that "**coolies**"—Chinese contract laborers—were a new form of slavery that enriched other Chinese. Congressional intentions behind restrictions on convicts and prostitutes were more nebulous. The law enforcement practices of the day did not allow immigration inspectors to determine whether an individual immigrant was undesirable. Instead, this law responded to a generalized public concern about the character of immigrants and gave immigration inspectors a tool by which to exclude immigrants, regardless of whether they were convicts or prostitutes. The antiprostitution provisions were, for example, a tool to exclude single women from immigration. Some immigration inspectors used these provisions rigorously, others not at all. In other words, potential immigrants faced varying treatment from port to port and from inspector to inspector. In practice, this law deterred few potential immigrants.

Congress strengthened the anti-Chinese provisions in 1882. In that year, it suspended the immigration of all Chinese laborers (though permitting the return migration of Chinese laborers already in the United States). It did permit the entry of Chinese students, teachers, merchants, and those "proceeding to the United States . . . from curiosity" (22 *Statutes at Large* 58, enacted May 6, 1882). The class bias in this law—excluding labor while admitting more elite Chinese—was soon to be applied to nationalities other than the Chinese.

In that same year, Congress established the first centralized control over immigration by establishing standards for state boards of immigration and added to the classes excluded from immigration. Persons likely to become a "public charge" could no longer immigrate. Congress also enacted a federal tax of fifty cents on alien passengers to the United States (22 *Statutes at Large* 214, enacted August 3, 1882).

In 1885, Congress extended the contract labor law from Asians to all nationalities. Henceforth, it was unlawful to import aliens to the United States for the performance of specific services of general labor for a specific length of time (23 *Statutes at Large* 332, enacted February 26, 1885). The exclusion of contract labor sought to reverse earlier patterns of labor immigration such as indentured servitude and contract labor. Again, this law was weakly enforced. European contract labor continued until the enactment of the Quota Acts in the early 1920s. In the Southwest, immigration of contract labor from Mexico continued into the 1960s and was managed by the U.S. government from 1943 to 1964 (the Bracero Program). To this day, some visas are available for short-term agricultural contract labor, particularly for labor in the citrus industry. Despite the erratic enforcement of the Contract Labor Law, it is important to understand that this provision in the immigration law sought to break one of the anchors of the immigrant flow—the pull of employment contracts and the expansion of labor recruitment into new areas of Europe that had not previously sent many immigrants to the United States.

These piecemeal efforts at immigration control declined after 1885. Taking their place were a series of increasingly restrictive comprehensive efforts at immigration control. In 1891, Congress passed the first comprehensive immigration control bill (26 *Statutes at Large* 1084, enacted March 3, 1891). The bill established a federal Bureau of Immigration to enforce immigration laws and expanded the excluded classes of immigrants to exclude individuals suffering from contagious diseases, polygamists, felons, individuals convicted of other crimes and misdemeanors, and aliens whose passages were paid by others (another stab at controlling labor recruitment). The law also forbade the encouragement of immigration by advertisement.

The second, third, and fourth comprehensive immigration control bills in 1903, 1907, and 1917, respectively, further limited immigrant access to the United States (32 *Statutes at Large* 1213, enacted March 3, 1903; 34 *Statutes at Large* 898, enacted February 20, 1907; and 39 *Statutes at Large* 874, enacted February 5, 1917). Newly excluded classes of immigrants included a virtual rogues' gallery of popular fears: anarchists, the illiterate, the feebleminded, those with physical or mental defects, children unaccompanied by their parents, and women coming to the United States for "immoral purposes." The establishment of the literacy requirement (in the 1917 bill) was the most sweeping of these changes. In this era, literacy was not the norm, particularly in those countries sending the lion's share of immigrants to the United States. Enforcement of this new literacy requirement slowed the immigration of Southern and Eastern Europeans as well as that of immigrants from Mexico and the Americas.

In these bills, Congress also mandated the **deportation** of immigrants who became public charges or were found, subsequent to immigration, to have any of the characteristics or beliefs that merited exclusion at immigration. In deportation, Congress identified a key enforcement tool for the assertion of federal authority. Prior to these laws, deportation was virtually unheard of for immigrants already residing in the United States, so once they had been admitted, their past was largely irrelevant. Even after the passage of the legislation, deportation was sparingly resorted to. Between 1908 and 1910, the United States deported an average of 2,300 immigrants annually. Despite the security concerns that surrounded World War I, this number increased to just 2,800 annually during the 1910s.

These piecemeal efforts at immigration control and the more comprehensive measures that followed shared a theme—excluding less desirable aliens from residence in the United States. Efforts such as these faced a problem, however. Enforcement rested with local authorities, mostly at ports in Eastern cities, who did not share the legislative concern about immigration. Thus, the specific exclusions did not have the impact desired by Congress, that is, the exclusion of poorer and less skilled immigrants (covered by specific exclusions for the illiterate, public charges, and contract laborers), as well as the ill, the infirm, and the radical.

The first decade of the twentieth century also saw the expansion of the nationalities excluded from immigration to the United States. In 1908, Japan and the United States negotiated the "Gentlemen's Agreement," under which Japan undertook to stop emigration to the United States. It entered into this agreement to avoid the outright exclusion that China suffered. By 1917, however, Congress passed legislation that excluded all Asians from immigration. Immigrants from this "barred zone" were inadmissible (39 *Statutes at Large* 874, enacted February 5, 1917).

These piecemeal policies increasingly failed to satisfy opponents of immigration. In an effort to develop a comprehensive immigration policy, Congress in 1907 created a commission to examine immigration. The commission, headed by Vermont's Senator William Dillingham, purported to have found that some nationalities—particularly those from Southern and Eastern Europe—were less assimilable than others and that those less likely to become good Americans should be excluded from immigration. Held up to today's standards for empirical research, the Dillingham Commission's methods were flawed, but in their day, they offered the intellectual justification to close America's doors to immigrants from some countries.

In the early 1920s, Congress crafted legislation that completed the United States' move away from open borders (42 *Statutes at Large* 5, enacted May 19, 1921; 43 *Statutes at Large* 153, enacted May 26, 1924). The Quota Acts of 1921 and 1924 were not as narrowly focused as the previous legislation had been. Instead, Congress established a virtual barricade against the national-origin populations that had increasingly dominated the immigrant flow in the early years of the twentieth century.

The Quota Acts established a national annual limit on immigration and allocated visas within this national limit based on the presence of foreign-born persons by country as measured in the 1910 census and (in the 1924 bill) in the 1890 census. These national-origin limits served to reinforce previously dominant national-origin patterns among immigrants. By using the 1890 census, Congress sought to exclude Southern and Eastern Europeans, who had begun to immigrate in large numbers after 1890. Congress also established a preference system for allocating the limited number of visas. Parents, spouses, and unmarried children of U.S. citizens were first in line. Perhaps most important, Congress mandated that immigrants had to have a visa issued by a U.S. consulate abroad at the time of entry. Thus, Congress limited which nationalities could immigrate and developed an effective enforcement mechanism to assure that local officials could not create their own policies. Congress also created a major exception to the quotas. Immigrants from countries in the Americas, including Mexico, could immigrate without numerical restriction, as long as they could meet other requirements such as being literate and not being likely to be a public charge.

Without realizing it, Congress created a new category of immigrant through the establishment of categories of immigrants ineligible to immigrate—the undocumented immigrant. These were immigrants residing in the United States who had entered without advance approval, who had entered despite having the characteristics or traits specifically prohibited among immigrants (nationality, illness, criminal record, or beliefs), or, in later years, those who had entered the United States on a temporary basis and had remained beyond the authorized period.

In these first years of immigration restriction, undocumented immigration was of only minor concern to Congress. In 1929, it passed **registry** legislation, which granted a presumption of legal status if an immigrant had been residing in the United States for eight years. This was the nation's first **legalization** program for undocumented immigrants. As demand for immigration increased and the categories of potential immigrants who were excluded from immigration eligibility grew, concern about undocumented immigration would also grow.

Federal Government Versus Local Government and Private Responsibility in Structuring U.S. Immigration.   In addition to the structuring of the immigrant flow that is evident in these growing restrictions, a second trend from this period needs to be noted. Increasingly, the federal government took responsibility for stimulating and regulating immigration and, in the process, diminished the role of private interests and local governments in shaping immigrant flows. When the borders were open, the federal government's sole role was to process immigrants at the ports. Incentives to immigration were private or local in nature, such as those offered by employers, shipping companies, states in the West seeking new population, or immigrants already in the United States seeking to encourage relatives or friends to immigrate.

Once the federal government began to address who could and could not immigrate, it became the focus of popular concerns about immigration. Thus, employers seeking a specific type of laborer—agricultural laborers, for example—could no longer simply recruit labor abroad. Instead, they had to convince lawmakers that the country needed agricultural labor (or they had to violate the law and recruit the undocumented). Similarly, immigrants seeking to assure that their relatives could immigrate to the United States had to assure that federal immigration laws respected the notion of family unification. Thus, as demand for immigration to the United States increased, Congress faced extensive pressures from diverse interests to expand immigration. Beginning in the 1960s, these demands reached fruition with the repeal of the Quota Acts.

Concern with immigration, however, was not limited to those seeking to expand the categories of individuals eligible to immigrate. Instead, popular opinion often opposed immigration or, at least, specific categories of immigration such as undocumented immigration. In sum, then, the process of establishing federal control over the borders introduced immigration as a national policy issue.

States and localities, however, continued to act autonomously in some cases. During the Great Depression, for example, states and cities in the Southwest deported large numbers of Mexican nationals and some U.S. citizens of Mexican ancestry (Balderama and Rodríguez 1995). As we will discuss in Chapter 4, states are attempting today to discourage immigration, particularly undocumented immigration, by making state employees such as teachers responsible for ascertaining the immigrant status of people seeking state services and by denying access to state social welfare benefits to the undocumented. Consequently, the assertion of federal responsibility over shaping immigrant flows remains open to debate. During periods of concern about immigration, states and localities seek a stronger role in deciding who should be admitted and who should be excluded.

Contemporary Immigration to the United States, 1965–1997

Today, the United States is experiencing another great wave of immigration. Each year, between 700,000 and 1 million immigrants enter the United States as permanent residents; they are supplemented by an estimated 300,000 undocumented immigrants. Immigration at this level is near the peak years of U.S. immigration in the early 1900s.

The statutory basis for this current wave of immigrants is a change made to U.S. immigration law in 1965 (79 *Statutes at Large* 911, enacted October 3, 1965). The **Immigration and Nationality Act of 1965** eliminated the national-origin quotas and established a new principle for U.S. immigration—**family unification**. Since the passage of the bill, annual levels of immigration—both documented and undocumented—have steadily increased. In addition to the dramatic increase in the number of immigrants, the 1965 act has facilitated a change in their countries of origin. The act, however, did not anticipate components of the immigrant stream that today vex policymakers, particularly undocumented immigrants and refugees/asylees. In the years since 1965, and most recently in 1996, Congress has amended the 1965 act and restricted the immigration opportunities of some who were eligible to immigrate under that act. These piecemeal changes, however, have failed to alter the 1965 act's liberal provisions for immigration. Although many observers expected that the 1996 immigration bill would fundamentally change U.S. immigration law, it did not. As we will show, the 1996 law did, however, enact provisions that will change the class composition of immigrants to the United States. This, in turn, will probably change the national-origin composition of immigrants to permanent residence.

The Statutory Foundation of Contemporary Immigration. The 1965 Immigration and Nationality Act eliminated the national-origin quotas that had been enacted in the 1920s. In their place, Congress established two categories of immigrants who would be welcomed. First, family members of U.S. citizens and permanent residents became eligible to immigrate. Family members, including spouses, children, parents, and siblings of U.S. citizens and permanent residents, made up about 80 percent of immigrants (this level has been reduced since 1990). Second, those with special occupational skills, abilities, or training could immigrate. These immigrants with job skills made up the remaining 20 percent of immigrants. The 1965 act established a permeable cap of 290,000 immigrants to the United States annually, with a limit for any single country of 20,000. These limits were permeable, however, because Congress made immediate relatives (spouses, minor children, and parents) exempt from these limitations.

Over the intervening three decades, the 1965 act has been amended several times to address three concerns. First, Congress has sought, largely unsuccessfully, to include the admission of refugees in the annual caps on immigration. Second, Congress has endeavored to control undocumented immigration. Finally, Congress has reexamined and reduced the preference for family unification in the 1965 immigration act.

The first of the pressures on immigration unanticipated by Congress in 1965 was a need to provide for the admission of refugees and asylees—individuals who had to leave their home countries in the face of persecution. Refugee/asylee admissions cannot be anticipated in advance; they occur during periods of political strife. As a result, immigration laws vest the power to award refugee status with the attorney general or, more broadly, with the executive branch. By vesting the power to admit refugees with the executive branch, immigration law is often placed in conflict with foreign policy objectives, with the executive branch usually responding to the pressures of foreign policy objectives to the disadvantage of an orderly refugee/asylee program. Immigration law seeks a regulated and predictable flow of immigrants with predefined traits or characteristics so that the immigrants do not come into conflict with U.S.-born populations; foreign policy seeks to strengthen the United States relative to its foes. Generally, when the two laws come into conflict, the United States has admitted as refugees the nationals of nations that the United States opposes, such as nationals of Communist states, while rejecting as refugees nationals of nations the United States supports. In the 1980s, for example, the United States readily admitted refugees from Nicaragua while rejecting nationals of El Salvador. The massive inflows of refugees of former Communist states, for instance, Cubans in the 1960s, 1970s, and early 1980s and Vietnamese in the mid-1970s, significantly altered the immigrant flow and created exactly the tensions with U.S.-born populations that the immigration law seeks to avoid. The rationale for this understanding of refugees was to admit political, but not economic, refugees. In practice, these distinctions have been impossible to make.

Congress's efforts to restructure refugee policy have not been successful. Beginning in 1980, refugees did not count against the annual limit in immigration so that regular immigration does not have to be reduced during periods of refugee admissions (94 *Statutes at Large* 102, enacted March 17, 1980). Congress has been unwilling to bar the admission of all refugees, but it has sought to cap the annual number of refugee admissions. However, these efforts conflict with the unpredictable nature of refugee immigration. Congress has also sought, in some cases, to negate executive branch denial of refugee status based on foreign policy considerations, such as linking the fate of Haitians and Cubans in 1994. Finally, in the

1996 immigration bill (discussed in greater depth later), Congress narrowed the standards for award of refugee status, required that individuals seeking asylee status apply within one year of arriving in the United States, sped the process for administrative review of refugee/asylee applications, and expedited the removal from the United States of individuals denied asylum. In general, however, immigration reform since 1965 has not significantly reduced executive branch authority over refugees and asylees.

The second element of immigration unanticipated in the 1965 act has proved even more vexing for Congress. This is the issue of undocumented immigration. When Congress reformed the immigration law in 1965, undocumented immigration existed, but it was not taken seriously by the public or policymakers. The undocumented immigrants of the era tended to be concentrated in the Southwest, and most were Mexican nationals working in U.S. agriculture. Also explaining policymakers' lack of concern in 1965 with undocumented immigration was a conscious effort by the Immigration and Naturalization Service to hide the problem. Using a federal government program designed to provide short-term agricultural labor—the Bracero Program—the INS periodically administratively legalized any undocumented immigrants from Mexico (Calavita 1992). Thus, in the late 1950s and early 1960s, when Congress became concerned about the problem, the INS would make it literally disappear. As a result, public outrage about undocumented immigrants that had swelled in the early 1950s was not present when Congress reformed immigration in 1965.

Beginning in the mid-1970s, however, policymakers and the general public grew to fear the level of undocumented immigration. For over a decade, Congress tried to craft a response. In 1986, it passed the **Immigration Reform and Control Act (IRCA)**. This act united the needs of diverse interests but in the end did little to slow undocumented immigration. It penalized the knowing employment of the undocumented and established a new requirement that citizenship or work eligibility be proven upon starting a new job (see Illustrations 2.2 and 2.3). Further, it gave permanent resident status to undocumented immigrants who had resided in the United States for at least five years and to undocumented immigrants with ninety days or more of work in perishable agriculture. Finally, it provided a means by which agricultural enterprises could recruit documented immigrants.

Although the act succeeded in legalizing the status of long-term undocumented immigrants already in the United States, it was unsuccessful in discouraging new undocumented immigrants from immigrating. Employers continued knowingly to hire undocumented immigrants. In part in response to pressures from employer organizations and chambers of commerce, the nation was unwill-

U.S. Department of Justice
Immigration and Naturalization Service

OMB No. 1115-0136
Employment Eligibility Verification

Please read instructions carefully before completing this form. The instructions must be available during completion of this form. ANTI-DISCRIMINATION NOTICE. It is illegal to discriminate against work eligible individuals. Employers CANNOT specify which document(s) they will accept from an employee. The refusal to hire an individual because of a future expiration date may also constitute illegal discrimination.

Section 1. Employee Information and Verification. To be completed and signed by employee at the time employment begins

Print Name: Last	First	Middle Initial	Maiden Name

Address *(Street Name and Number)*	Apt. #	Date of Birth *(month/day/year)*

City	State	Zip Code	Social Security #

I am aware that federal law provides for imprisonment and/or fines for false statements or use of false documents in connection with the completion of this form.	I attest, under penalty of perjury, that I am (check one of the following): A citizen or national of the United States A Lawful Permanent Resident (Alien # A_____) An alien authorized to work until___/___/___ (Alien # or Admission #_____)

Employee's Signature	Date *(month/day/year)*

Preparer and/or Translator Certification. *(To be completed and signed if Section 1 is prepared by a person other than the employee.) I attest, under penalty of perjury, that I have assisted in the completion of this form and that to the best of my knowledge the information is true and correct.*

Preparer's/Translator's Signature	Print Name

Address *(Street Name and Number, City, State, Zip Code)*	Date *(month/day/year)*

Section 2. Employer Review and Verification. To be completed and signed by employer. Examine one document from List A OR examine one document from List B **and** one from List C as listed on the reverse of this form and record the title, number and expiration date, if any, of the document(s)

List A	OR	List B	AND	List C
Document title: _____		_____		_____
Issuing authority: _____		_____		_____
Document #: _____		_____		_____
Expiration Date *(if any)*: _/_/_		_/_/_		_/_/_
Document #: _____				
Expiration Date *(if any)*: _/_/_				

CERTIFICATION - I attest, under penalty of perjury, that I have examined the document(s) presented by the above-named employee, that the above-listed document(s) appear to be genuine and to relate to the employee named, that the employee began employment on *(month/day/year)* __/__/__ and that to the best of my knowledge the employee is eligible to work in the United States. (State employment agencies may omit the date the employee began employment).

Signature of Employer or Authorized Representative	Print Name	Title

Business or Organization Name	Address *(Street Name and Number, City, State, Zip Code)*	Date *(month/day/year)*

Section 3. Updating and Reverification. To be completed and signed by employer

A. New Name *(if applicable)*	B. Date of rehire *(month/day/year) (if applicable)*

C. If employee's previous grant of work authorization has expired, provide the information below for the document that establishes current employment eligibility.

Document   Title:_____Document   #:_____Expiration   Date   (if   any):__/__/__

I attest, under penalty of perjury, that to the best of my knowledge, this employee is eligible to work in the United States, and if the employee presented document(s), the document(s) I have examined appear to be genuine and to relate to the individual.

Signature of Employer or Authorized Representative	Date *(month/day/year)*

Form I-9 (Rev. 11-21-91) N

ILLUSTRATION 2.2   An I-9 Form to Verify Work Eligibility

ing and unable to enforce the employer sanctions provisions of the act. Certainly, some employers were fined for hiring the undocumented. Few, however, were jailed. Congress drafted the law in such a way as to offer employers an easy excuse. As long as they had no reason to believe that the documents that new employees presented were false, they could not be prosecuted for employing the undocu-

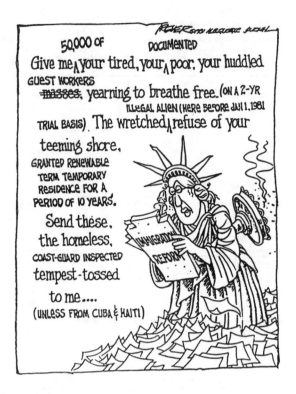

ILLUSTRATION 2.3
Complexity, or the Immigration Reform and Control Act. Reprinted by permission of John Trever, *Albuquerque Journal.*

mented. A plethora of false documents and employer ignorance combined to assure that little changed after the IRCA was passed.

In the early 1990s, Congress and the executive branch vigorously pursued a new strategy: vastly increasing appropriations to the INS, particularly to the INS border control operations. Between 1993 and 1996, for example, the INS budget increased by 68 percent. The Clinton administration's budget requests (which Congress has been exceeding) are projected between 1993 and 1998 to more than double the INS budget. In this same period, the number of border guards is projected to increase by 85 percent. This increase in funding has increased the number of apprehensions—undocumented immigrants caught along the border or in work sites—but there is no evidence that it has slowed the pace of undocumented immigration; it has just made it more difficult and costly.

In 1996, Congress again revisited policy toward undocumented immigration. In addition to continuing the pattern of adding to INS resources and expanding the border patrol, Congress sought to create a new disincentive to undocumented migration. Beginning in 1997, undocumented immigrants in the United States who are caught will not be able to receive a permanent resident visa for a minimum of three years after returning to their home country. Just as this provision of the law was to be implemented for the first time, Congress delayed its implementation and debated removing it completely from the law. As many as one-third of new permanent residents had previously resided in the United States as undocumented immigrants. The 1996 bill also sought to speed the deportation of undocumented immigrants and non-naturalized immigrants convicted of committing a felony.

Since the passage of the 1965 immigration bill, Congress has also reexamined the level and composition of annual immigration to the United States. The same legislation that sought to guarantee the admission of refugees also reduced to 270,000 the number of other **preference immigrants** to be admitted annually. Preference immigrants are those other than immediate family members of U.S. citizens.

Congress again addressed the issue of immigrant numbers in 1990 (104 *Statutes at Large* 4978, enacted November 29, 1990). The annual target number of immigrants was raised to 675,000. Although this may appear to be an increase, it simply reflects more accurately the level of nonpreference immigration. Again, this was a permeable cap, with immediate family members exempt from numerical limitations. The 1990 bill also reallocated the share of visas dedicated to family unification and employment-related visas. Congress reduced the share of visas allocated to family members to approximately 70 percent of the total and held the share for employment visas to 20 percent. The remaining visas go into a new category called, somewhat disingenuously, "**diversity visas**." The diversity visas are available to nationals of countries that have not made up a large share of recent immigrants. These diversity immigrants have come mostly from Europe. Since these immigrants do not have the connection to the United States that others do (either family members or job skills desired by employers), the visas are awarded at random through a mail-in lottery. Once these diversity immigrants are here, however, they may begin to petition for the immigration of their relatives. Thus, the diversity program simply creates new streams for future preference and nonpreference family unification immigration.

In the period leading up to the vote on the 1996 immigration bill, many analysts expected more than an incremental reform. These expectations emerged because of the rise in mass interest in immigration that began with California's approval of **Proposition 187** and the advocacy of reduced levels of immigration by prominent national leaders of both parties. During the year leading up to congressional consideration of this bill, it seemed quite likely that Congress would enact legislation that would cap the number of immigrants at a level lower than average immigration in the early 1990s, perhaps at levels significantly below the then current levels.

The bill that Congress passed—the Illegal Immigration Reform and Immigrant Responsibility Act of 1996—proved to fit better with the pattern of incremental reform. It included no cap on immigration to permanent residence. Its focus was more on enhanced border enforcement than on immigration to permanent residence.

One section of the bill will, however, change the composition of contemporary immigration. The bill tightens the requirements for immigrant sponsors. The **sponsor** is the U.S. citizen or permanent resident who petitions for the immigration of a foreign national. The sponsor promises to take financial responsibility for the immigrant during the first few years of residence. Prior to the passage of the 1996 law, this promise meant little and only applied during the first three to five years of the immigrant's residence.

The 1996 bill changed these responsibilities in three ways. First, Congress established a minimum income level for the sponsor—125 percent of the poverty level for the sponsor, the sponsor's family, and the immigrant being sponsored. Second, it made the sponsorship legally enforceable, so the sponsor could not subsequently abandon the immigrant. States could take the sponsor's income into account when deciding whether the immigrant was eligible for benefit programs targeted at the poor. Finally, it extended the duration of the sponsorship to ten years (or until the immigrant naturalizes, if that occurs before ten years).

Of these changes, the first will have the most dramatic impact. The household income of the petitioner must be 125 percent of the poverty level for a family the size of the petitioner's plus the immigrant (or the immigrant's family if the petition is for an entire family). Thus, if the petitioner has a family of four and seeks the admission of an immigrant, the combined "family" income of the petitioner, the petitioner's family, and the immigrant must exceed approximately $20,000 (at 1994 levels). Larger petitioner families (or petitions for immigrant families) would raise the required level of "family" income by $2,250 (in 1994 dollars) per family member. These provisions add a class dynamic that was not present for family preference immigrants (the nature of allocating employment preference visas was always to reward the skilled and the educated). Prior to 1996, immigration eligibility was established through blood, skills, or randomness. These changes add a new factor—income. The likely result is that fewer family preference immigrants from Mexico, the Dominican Republic, and, perhaps, the Philippines will be able to meet the qualifications for the award of a visa.

In 1996, Congress also reformed welfare by limiting access of immigrants to federal social welfare programs. We discuss the question of the relationship of the state to immigrants in greater depth in Chapters 3 and 4. For now, however, it is important to note that Congress is seeking to diminish immigrant access to government benefits. It is unclear, however, whether this would act as a significant disincentive to immigration.

The Composition of Contemporary Immigration.   There have been a number of consequences of the 1965 act. First, it has encouraged steadily increasing levels of immigration. Second, it has concentrated access to immigration to nationals of those countries that have recently sent immigrants to the United States (as the previous immigrants offer access to immigration visas to their relatives). Finally, as it limits immigration for many who desire access to the United States and simultaneously allows large numbers to immigrate, it creates an incentive to undocumented immigration as well as large legal immigrant communities into which undocumented immigrants can merge and, in many cases, disappear.

Between 1965 and 1996, 20.1 million people immigrated to the United States as permanent residents. Although current annual levels of immigration are below those recorded in the first decade of this century, the high annual levels of immigration in the current wave have lasted much longer than the years of highest immigration during the Second Great Wave. In the 1970s, annual immigration averaged almost 500,000 per year and grew to over 700,000 per year in the 1980s (some of these 1980s immigrants were the previously undocumented who legalized under the Immigration Reform and Control Act). In the 1990s, annual immigration has numbered between 800,000 and 1 million per year. Although these levels are high by historical standards, the immigrants enter a United States that is much larger than it was at the turn of the century. Today, 900,000 immigrants would constitute just three-tenths of 1 percent of the national population. The same 900,000 immigrants added 1 percent to the nation's 92 million residents in 1910. Thus, depending on the measure, immigration can be seen as being at a record high or at just moderately high levels. As we have seen in other eras of U.S. immigration history, raw numbers are not necessarily the factors that generate concern about immigration among the U.S.-born population. Instead, concerns arise from perceptions of economic or cultural challenge as well as from fears that immigrants are not adapting adequately to life in the United States.

These approximately 900,000 immigrants are not randomly selected from throughout the world. Although the 1965 act and its successors reversed the racist elements of the Quota Acts, they did not assure unfettered immigration to the United States. Instead, the immigration law rewards foreign nationals who have immediate relatives in the United States (as well as those with job skills). The consequence of the family preference bias in immigration law is that some nationalities dominate the contemporary immigrant flow (see Table 2.4).

TABLE 2.4   Regions and Countries of Origin of Permanent Resident Immigrants, 1951–1995

Region	1951– 1960	1961– 1970	1971– 1980	1981– 1990[a]	1991– 1995[a]
Europe	1,325,727	1,123,492	800,368	761,550	764,835
Latin America and					
the Caribbean	605,681	1,193,645	1,618,884	3,111,760	2,625,982
Asia	153,249	427,642	1,588,178	2,738,157	1,574,817
Africa	14,092	28,954	80,779	176,893	148,463
Oceania	12,976	25,122	41,242	45,205	30,318
Countries:					
Latin America					
Mexico	299,811	453,937	640,294	1,655,843	1,490,153
Cuba	78,948	108,536	264,863	144,578	65,217
Dominican					
Republic	9,897	93,292	148,135	252,035	218,548
El Salvador	5,895	14,992	34,436	213,539	129,133
Argentina	19,486	49,721	29,897	27,327	15,999
Colombia	18,048	72,028	77,347	122,849	66,048
Ecuador	9,841	36,780	50,077	56,315	37,080
Asia					
China[b]	9,657	34,764	124,326	346,747	211,303
India	1,973	27,189	164,134	250,786	182,434
Korea	6,231	34,526	267,638	333,746	91,954
Philippines	19,307	98,376	354,987	548,764	298,162

[a]Data from the 1980s and early 1990s include immigrants legalized under the Immigration Reform and Control Act of 1986.

[b]After 1957, data for China include Taiwan. China data do not include Hong Kong.

Source: Authors' compilations based on U.S. Immigration and Naturalization Service, 1994, table 2; and U.S. Immigration and Naturalization Service, 1997, table 2.

A quick review of the history of U.S. immigration demonstrates that a few countries have always dominated a period's immigration. Today, however, this phenomenon is a by-product of law and not a function of private initiatives and the availability of transportation. Unless the law is changed, the countries that have dominated the flow in recent years—such as Mexico, the Philippines, and the Dominican Republic—will continue to as long as there is demand for immigrant visas in those countries.

Under the 1965 act, two regions have overwhelmingly dominated the immigration flow. Asia and Latin America made up 84 percent of immigrants in the first three years of this decade. This Asian and Latin American share increased from 58 percent in the 1960s.

Contemporary immigrants are slightly more likely to be men than women, though in some years the proportion of women is greater. Approximately three-fourths of immigrants have relatives residing in the United States. Approximately one-third of "new" immigrants already resided in the United States, either as temporary visitors, holders of nonpermanent work or student visas, or in an undocumented status. One-fourth of immigrants are younger than twenty years of age and 5 percent are sixty-five or older.

Just as these immigrants do not immigrate evenly from throughout the world, they do not settle evenly throughout the United States. As they have from the nation's first days, immigrants disproportionately settle in cities. Even among cities, the most likely destinations are those near borders and those with the most extensive international air links. Thus, cities such as Los Angeles, New York, Miami, Houston, and Chicago are the homes to more immigrants than Kansas City, Minneapolis, or Seattle. In 1993, for example, more than 25 percent of new immigrants reported that they intended to reside in just two cities—New York and Los Angeles—and just 5 percent of immigrants reported that they would reside in rural areas (U.S. Immigration and Naturalization Service 1994, table 19). Several states also bear the brunt of new immigration. Almost two-thirds of 1993 immigrants intended to reside in five states—California, New York, Texas, Florida, and New Jersey.

The diversity of today's immigrants to permanent residence makes it difficult to generalize about their economic and social opportunities. The modal immigrant experience limits the occupational opportunity and the immigrant life primarily to involvement around other immigrants, many of whom are coethnics. The factory jobs that allowed the immigrants of the Second Great Wave and their children and grandchildren to move up in society have largely disappeared. In their place are service sector and other low-skill jobs that do not offer extensive opportunities for economic advancement. Immigrant households, however, overcome these limitations by having multiple wage earners who often hold multiple jobs. In addition to these high levels of labor force participation, immigrant households have higher savings rates than comparably situated U.S.-born households.

The decline of factory employment and unionized labor does not just affect immigrants. U.S.-born citizens with low levels of education or job skills are disadvantaged as well by these changes in the economy. The important point to consider when relating this change in the economy to immigrants is that the nature of employment and the range of opportunities have changed considerably since the last period of high levels of immigration. Thus, it is not possible to say that since previous immigrants were able to become successful and contributing members of the economy, today's immigrants can as well. Whether they will be able to or not, then, is an unanswerable issue.

One opportunity available to immigrant households that has improved since the turn of the century is public education. The ethos of opportunity that drives immigrants to hold multiple jobs appears to extend to their children. Language difficulties as well as the decline in urban public education, however, raise a question as to how immigrant children, no matter how motivated, will be able to take full advantage of this opportunity.

It is inaccurate to paint contemporary immigrants with a single brush. The United States also attracts many highly skilled immigrants seeking better wages or living conditions than are available in their countries of origin. For example, many immigrants from India arrive with medical degrees and many from the Philippines are registered nurses. Other nations send large numbers of professionals each year. This heterogeneity in the skills and resources of contemporary immigrants is often lost in discussions of immigrant contributions to U.S. society.

When we began this discussion of immigrant economic and social opportunities, we cautioned that the diversity of today's immigrants makes it impossible to generalize about their experiences. Some immigrants, and even immigrant communities, have achieved a great deal of economic success and social prestige. In some cases, this simply reflects that individual immigrants brought wealth with them when they immigrated. For example, Rupert Murdoch, the president of News World Communications, became a naturalized citizen, at least in part so that he could purchase U.S. television stations. He is hardly an American success story, though he has certainly prospered here. A more interesting case is offered by the immigrant populations that have formed self-reinforcing economic identities, or "**enclaves**," that allow the immigrant-ethnic community as a whole to prosper. In these enclaves, which have appeared in the Cuban, Chinese, and Korean immigrant communities of some cities, immigrants work for coethnic immigrant-owned businesses, patronize stores owned by coethnics, and generally live in an economic world revolving around coethnics. Thus, resources stay within the immigrant-ethnic population and help to build the community. These businesses employ new coethnic immigrants and offer them opportunities disproportionate to those they would encounter outside of the ethnic community. Enclaves do not form automatically. Discrimination by the dominant society is a key initial incentive for entrepreneurs to look within the ethnic community economically. And the enclave is no guarantee of success. Communities without any resources would not be advantaged by only looking within, yet they offer a tool for immigrant communities to grow economically despite changes in the national economy and in public education.

So far, this discussion of contemporary immigration has neglected a key component—undocumented immigration. According to the best estimates, approximately 300,000 undocumented immigrants immigrate to the United States each year. As these are people who do not wish to be counted, this figure can only be an estimate, subject to a great deal of controversy. It is simply not possible to say how many of these undocumented immigrants remain in the United States for extensive periods.

Like the permanent resident population, the undocumented are unevenly distributed nationally. The one concrete state-level estimate suggests that 40 percent of the 5 million undocumented immigrants who resided in the United States in October 1996 lived in California (see Table 2.5). Other states having more than 100,000 undocumented immigrants were New York, Texas, Florida, Illinois, New Jersey, and Arizona.

The national origins of these undocumented immigrants are slightly more diverse than their states of residence. Mexico provides the largest number, approximately 2.7 million. Of the other countries in the top twenty providers of undocumented immigrants, nine were Latin American, four were in the English-speaking Caribbean, and four were Asian.

The economic and social opportunities available to the undocumented are less well known than those available to permanent residents. As late as the 1960s, most undocumented immigrants worked in agriculture. Increasingly, however, the undocumented population has moved into urban areas. The available jobs tend to be those offering the fewest protections. Although the research is not comprehensive, the labor market opportunities include day labor, construction, textiles, and service sector work. As risks exist for employing the undocumented, they are more likely to be employed by smaller firms rather than larger firms, and these smaller firms are less likely to offer benefits. Because of their status, undocumented immigrants also face a greater likelihood of working for employers who violate U.S. labor laws, particularly minimum wage and overtime laws. Increasingly, there is also evidence of employers who imprison undocumented immigrants and create conditions reminiscent of slavery.

Finally, the undocumented do not compose a distinct population separate from the permanent residents. Many immigrant households include both permanent residents and undocumented immigrants. The undocumented in these households are waiting for permanent resident visas, although the wait may be one of many years (and impossible, in reality). Thus, the two immigrant populations overlap in many ways in major metropolitan areas.

TABLE 2.5 Undocumented Immigrant Population by Country of Origin and by State, October 1996

Country of Origin		Population
1.	Mexico	2,700,000
2.	El Salvador	335,000
3.	Guatemala	165,000
4.	Canada	120,000
5.	Haiti	105,000
6.	Philippines	95,000
7.	Honduras	90,000
8.	Poland	70,000
8.	Nicaragua	70,000
8.	Bahamas	70,000
11.	Colombia	65,000
12.	Ecuador	55,000
13.	Dominican Republic	50,000
13.	Trinidad and Tobago	50,000
13.	Jamaica	50,000
16.	Pakistan	41,000
17.	India	33,000
18.	Dominica	32,000
19.	Peru	30,000
19.	Korea	30,000
	Other countries	744,000
	Total	5,000,000

State		Population
1.	California	2,000,000
2.	Texas	700,000
3.	New York	540,000
4.	Florida	350,000
5.	Illinois	290,000
6.	New Jersey	135,000
7.	Arizona	115,000
8.	Massachusetts	85,000
9.	Virginia	55,000
10.	Washington	52,000
11.	Colorado	45,000
12.	Maryland	44,000
13.	Michigan	37,000

(continues)

TABLE 2.5 *(continued)*

State	Population
13. Pennsylvania	37,000
13. New Mexico	37,000
16. Oregon	33,000
17. Georgia	32,000
18. District of Columbia	30,000
19. Connecticut	29,000
20. Nevada	24,000
Other states	330,000
Total	5,000,000

Source: U.S. Immigration and Naturalization Service, 1997, table P.

Assuming that the estimate of approximately 5 million undocumented immigrants is accurate, there are many fewer undocumented immigrants than there are permanent residents—no more than one undocumented immigrant for every three permanent residents. In the public mind, however, most immigrants are undocumented immigrants (see Chapter 5).

Not surprisingly, the areas of high immigrant concentration are the ones where the greatest conflict occurs between immigrants and the U.S.-born. The roots of the **English-Only movement** (an effort to promote English as the "official" language of the jurisdiction) were in Miami, where Cuban immigrants and U.S.-born whites were in conflict over culture and language. California, which has received more immigrants than any other state, spurred the current national consideration of immigration restriction with its approval of Proposition 187.

Proposition 187, which was held to be largely unconstitutional in late 1997 and was not implemented for the most part, sought to deny social welfare and education benefits to the undocumented and to the U.S.-citizen children of the undocumented. Voter support for this proposition suggests two important lessons about the contemporary concern about immigration. The proposition received its highest levels of support from parts of California with few immigrants. Thus, like the support for the American Know-Nothing Party in the 1850s, opposition to immigrants does not come from those who have direct contact with them. Instead, it is those more removed from immigrants who perceive that the quality of their lives is worsened by immigrants. In today's California, the concern of the proposition's supporters relates to the cost of providing services to immigrants. The second lesson of Proposition 187 is that the engine of the concern about immigration is not their labor. California has long sought the labor of the undocumented. Instead, the impetus comes from the provision of services, particularly education and health care. Thus, the undocumented immigrant is an easy target for those who seek to change the relationship between the government and the people. We return to this topic in Chapter 4.

Reforming Immigration

The dramatic changes to the volume and composition of U.S. immigration resulting from the 1965 immigration act have raised concerns among many policymakers and many citizens that the immigration law must again be changed. The United States is again debating what we have identified as the central dilemma in immigration policy: how many immigrants the nation should admit and what characteristics they should have. Although the specifics are unclear, there appears to be a widely held view that the overall level of immigration should be reduced and that the present composition of immigration should change. There is less consensus on what the composition should change to.

Proposed Changes Concerning Immigration to Permanent Residence

Broadly, the two types of changes that may occur in immigration restate the dilemma raised in the introduction to this chapter—the overall numbers of immigrants and the characteristics that these immigrants bring with them. Although Congress will probably not specifically address the question of changing the national-origin composition of legal immigrants to the United States, it may well change as a consequence of the other two changes.

As noted earlier, immigration in the early 1990s numbered between 800,000 and 1 million annually. In 1996, Congress considered and rejected proposals that would reduce these levels to between 200,000 and 500,000 annually and that would limit the family members eligible for immigration. Public opinion polling, however, indicates that there is a broad public consensus supporting reduced immigration, so these proposals will likely be considered again (Espenshade and Hempstead 1996; de la Garza and DeSipio forthcoming). Some prominent national leaders—including perennial Republican presidential candidate Patrick Buchanan—have called for a five-year moratorium on all immigration. Advocates of maintaining current levels of immigration can accomplish their goal by blocking any major change to U.S. immigration law. This is what happened in 1996.

Any reduction in immigration would disproportionately affect the countries that provide the highest numbers of immigrants. As we have suggested, the family preference system raises the likelihood of immigration of those who have immediate relatives in the United States. This happens only among national-origin populations that have recent immigrants among their numbers. To the extent that these family preference immigrants would be replaced by immigrants with specific skills or education, this change would increase the share of immigrants coming from countries sending skilled professionals to the United States. Thus, proposals to reduce the family preference share of the immigrant pool would reduce the share of Latin American immigrants, particularly Mexicans and Dominicans, and increase the share of immigrants coming from Europe. Although the numbers of immigrants from some parts of Asia would decline—from the Philippines and Vietnam, particularly—the share coming from other parts of Asia would rise.

In sum, the current reform proposals seek to reduce the overall number of annual immigrants and to shift slightly the allocation of visas within that overall limit from family unification to individuals with specific skills. If enacted, these proposals would slow the number of immigrants admitted annually and would alter the national-origin makeup of today's immigration. Any new reforms will add to the impact of the new sponsorship standards established in 1996. This new class bias will shape immigration. Although class has certainly been an element in previous immigration laws (such as the Chinese "proceeding to the United States . . . from curiosity"), this provision makes all immigrants subject to a class test.

Proposed Legislative Solutions to Undocumented Immigration

Individual members of Congress have also proposed strategies to address undocumented immigration, and as a body, Congress seems more interested in passing some legislation on undocumented immigration than it is on legal immigration. There is, however, no comprehensive proposal or set of proposals with widespread support to address this issue. Instead, the failure of the Immigration Reform and Control Act has made Congress shy about seeking a new comprehensive legislative solution. Instead, Congress is seeking to pass legislation with piecemeal solutions and enhancements of current law.

First, Congress has added significantly to the appropriations for border control and enforcement by the Immigration and Naturalization Service. These funds have allowed the INS to experiment with new border control strategies. The most favored of these is saturating key stretches of the border with guards on a continuing basis. These strategies—modeled on El Paso's "**Operation Hold the Line**"— are not overwhelmingly successful because immigrants can select an alternative route to a crossing where the INS is not watching. Further, these labor-intensive strategies are very expensive to implement and maintain. Their major effect is limiting the number of undocumented immigrants seeking to cross the border for a day job or to make purchases in the United States, thus these strategies often hurt merchants and businesses in the border community. Immigrants seeking a longer-term residence in the United States continue to find routes around the enhanced enforcement.

Second, Congress is seeking to limit undocumented immigrant access to state and local benefits, particularly education services for children. Although proposals to deny education to undocumented children would seem to reverse the Supreme Court's ruling in *Plyler v. Doe*, the Court in that ruling held open the possibility that the national government could do what it said the states could not—that is, deny education to undocumented children. Congress rejected any such efforts in 1996.

Several possible long-term solutions have been offered to address undocumented immigration, but Congress has been unwilling to examine options other than increased enforcement. The most prominent of these suggestions is the establishment of a national identification card that is fraud-proof. Objections to this are raised on both the political left and right. Civil libertarians are concerned that the identification card could come to be required for all activities, not just employment, and could be used to monitor people's activities. Immigrant advocates fear that the identification would be required of minorities and might offer an excuse to employers not to consider employing Latinos or Asians, regardless of their citizenship or work eligibility status. Employers, particularly small-business owners, are concerned that a new identification requirement would add to the regulatory paperwork burdens. These concerns have been sufficiently widespread and diverse in origin to limit congressional interest. It is unclear how long they will outweigh national concern about the undocumented.

Conclusion

The fundamental dilemma in U.S. immigration policy has not been resolved and probably never will be. Instead, each generation will decide how many immigrants should be admitted and what characteristics they should have. The trend through the twentieth century has been to admit ever more immigrants but to be selective about what traits these immigrants should have, with immediate or blood relationship to a U.S. citizen or permanent resident being of greatest value after 1965. Although the public today supports reducing the overall number of immigrants, this popular consensus will come into conflict with the economy's demand for immigrant labor (a theme we return to in Chapter 5). If history is a model, it will take years of popular opposition to immigration before Congress acts. As has been true throughout the history of immigration to the United States, immigrants are respected enough for popular opposition to immigration to be held at bay.

Whatever the outcome of this debate, it is now resolved that the federal government will design and implement the new policy, particularly when it concerns immigration to permanent residence. The twentieth century has seen a centralization of the control of immigration policy in the federal government. In terms of control over immigration to permanent residence, the federal government both shapes and implements policy. These policies often conflict with other federal objectives, but the states are not given the opportunity to impose themselves in these vacuums. Instead, federal immigration policy is often subordinated to other federal programs. It is in the area of undocumented immigration, however, that states are seeking a new role. Following the lead of California and its Proposition 187, states are seeking to discourage undocumented immigration. In this regard, the states are filling a void in which the federal government has not been able to implement its policies successfully. As we will suggest in Chapter 4, however, the state policies are potentially no more effective than the federal government's weak implementation of the Immigration Reform and Control Act and its inability to control the borders.

Thus, although Washington has centralized control over immigration, it has never been in a position to dominate the economy's demand for immigrant labor. Moreover, concern about immigration has never overcome reverence for immigrants.

3

Making Americans:
U.S. Naturalization Policy

T HAT THE UNITED STATES IS A NATION OF IMMIGRANTS is undeniable. Throughout the nation's history, wave after wave of immigrants has populated the land, diversified the population, and kindled the economy. A final impact has been more muted though no less revolutionary. By their presence, immigrants have challenged the nation to meet its commitment to democracy and equal opportunity by incorporating their voices into the nation's politics.

With notable and sorry exceptions, immigrant desire for incorporation has been met over the past two hundred years. Throughout the nation's history, immigrants (and, more recently, legal immigrants) have been eligible to naturalize as U.S. citizens and acquire a legal status virtually indistinguishable from that of the U.S.-born. The only limitations on the naturalized are that they may not serve as either president or vice president and that they are subject to the loss of citizenship through denaturalization if it can be proved that the applicant lied in the application for naturalization. In practice, however, naturalized citizens rarely face denaturalization.

Today, the nation is adding a record number of new citizens through naturalization (see Table 3.1). We estimate, for example, that in the 1990s, between 5 and 7 million immigrants will decide to become U.S. citizens. They will account for approximately 13 percent of the increase in U.S. citizens in the 1990s (the remainder will achieve citizenship through birth in the United States or by birth abroad to U.S. citizen parents). Nonetheless, it is important to note that immigrants are slow to naturalize. In only two decades of the twentieth century (the 1930s and 1940s) has naturalization exceeded immigration.

This gap between immigration and naturalization creates potential tensions for the polity as well as for the immigrant. Simply stated, the polity faces the twin dilemmas of which immigrants to incorporate and on what terms. When policymakers have addressed this first dilemma, they have had to confront the questions of who should be eligible to naturalize, what characteristics naturalized citizens should have, and, as was the case with immigration policy, what level of government should administer the transition from denizen to citizen. These three policy conflicts—who, what characteristics, and which government level—echo through the two hundred years of U.S. naturalization history. We examine each of these conflicts in turn in this chapter. Although each is a policy question in its own right,

TABLE 3.1   Immigration and Naturalization, 1907–2000

	Immigration	*Naturalization*
1907[a]–1910	3,861,575	111,738
1911–1920	5,735,811	1,128,972
1921–1930	4,107,209	1,173,185
1931–1940	528,431	1,518,464
1941–1950	1,035,039	1,987,028
1951–1960	2,515,479	1,189,946
1961–1970	3,321,677	1,120,263
1971–1980	4,493,314	1,464,772
1981–1990[b]	7,338,062	2,375,727
1991–1995[b]	5,230,313	1,716,242
1991–2000 (estimate)	9,981,000[c]	5,466,000[d]

[a]The federal government did not collect naturalization data prior to 1907.

[b]Immigration data include immigrants who legalized under the Immigration Reform and Control Act of 1986. These immigrants began to be eligible for naturalization in 1993.

[c]Estimate for 1990s immigration based on 1991–1995 non-IRCA legalization immigrations plus the number of legalization beneficiaries 1991–1995.

[d]Estimate for the 1990s naturalization derived from naturalizations in 1991 through 1995 and applications received by the Immigration and Naturalization Service in 1996. An estimate based on the average number of naturalizations over the past decade indicates that 2,558,303 immigrants will naturalize in the 1990s.

Source: U.S. Immigration and Naturalization Service, 1994, table 4; U.S. Immigration and Naturalization Service, 1997, table 1 and 44.

it is important to see that together they are components of the larger dilemma in U.S. naturalization policy—which immigrants to incorporate as citizens.

Naturalization also involves an individual decision made by all immigrants, specifically to pledge loyalty or attachment to the sending country or to the United States. Throughout U.S. history, most immigrants have developed loyalty to the United States and many have thereupon sought citizenship, a pattern that continues today. Still, attainment of citizenship varies between different nationalities. In this chapter, we examine the individual and group determinants of naturalization as a backdrop to the second dilemma in naturalization policy—on what terms the nation should incorporate its voluntary citizens.

Traditionally, the United States has offered little encouragement to immigrants to naturalize but has willingly accepted them when they have sought to join the polity. In this voluntary system, some groups of immigrants have been more likely to seek membership than others. To the extent that these differences reflect varied levels of individual desire for citizenship, the state faces a dilemma only if a distinct immigrant population rejects American political values, yet stays in the United States. There is no contemporary or historical evidence to suggest that definable groups of immigrants have rejected the American political system in this way. If the differential rates of citizenship attainment, however, reflect varying impediments faced by immigrants based on nationality or some other trait, then these differential rates of nationalization raise a serious dilemma for the polity. We also examine the individual and group determinants of naturalization in this chapter.

These two dilemmas—whom the nation should admit as citizens and on what terms—appear in various forms throughout the history of U.S. naturalization. As we will show, policymakers have responded to these dilemmas differently in different eras, and the specific policies debated to address these dilemmas have differed. These traditional dilemmas, like the dilemma surrounding immigration policy, have not been finally resolved, nor will they be as long as the United States remains a nation of immigrants.

Naturalization as a National Policy

Among the few powers explicitly reserved in the Constitution for the federal government is that of naturalization. Despite the absence of an explicit conception of national (as opposed to state) citizenship at the time of the nation's founding, the founding fathers assured that the national government would retain control of naturalization. Article 1, Section 8 of the Constitution grants Congress the power "to establish a uniform rule of naturalization."

The constitutional mandate to vest naturalization powers with the national government may be seen as part of a broad effort to guarantee that the federal government would be able to assure continued national growth. Had naturalization powers rested with the states, states not wishing to receive immigrants could have developed restrictive naturalization rules. Further, states might have used naturalization powers to limit immigrant access to *state* citizenship, which offered more tangible benefits at the time of the drafting of the Constitution. Either of these outcomes could have slowed the potential for growth of the United States.

The roots of these concerns about the consequences of restrictive naturalization policies can be found in the immediate prerevolutionary period. The Declaration of Independence offers an insight. As noted in Chapter 2, among the charges against King George III was this: "He has endeavored to prevent the population of these states; for that purpose obstructing the laws for naturalization of foreigners; refusing to pass others to encourage their migrations hither, and raising the conditions of new appropriations of lands."

The first Congress quickly seized the constitutional mandate and developed an outline for naturalization requirements that has survived for the past two hundred years. With the benefit of hindsight, we see that the constitutional provision of national control over naturalization has had the desired impact. With a brief four-year exception early in the nation's history, most immigrants have been assured of a relatively quick transition to citizenship. Although Congress has added individual skill and knowledge requirements in the twentieth century, we will argue that these too have been relatively minimal and do not offer an insurmountable impediment for immigrants seeking citizenship. Thus, despite periodic local passions against immigrants, the United States has consistently provided immigrants with a path to citizenship. Instead of focusing, then, on the question of whether immigrants *should* have access to citizenship, policymakers have addressed who should be offered citizenship and who should administer their transition from immigrant to citizen.

Who Should Be Offered U.S. Citizenship?

Over the past two hundred years, U.S. naturalization law has examined the question of who should be offered U.S. citizenship in two ways. The first involves the categories of immigrants to be offered U.S. citizenship (what we call the "who" question). The second concerns the characteristics and abilities that individuals within these categories need to have to be eligible for naturalization (what we identify as "which characteristics"). For the first one hundred and sixty years of U.S. naturalization history, the first of these questions—the "who" issue—was Congress's primary concern. Beginning at the turn of the twentieth century, however, the second issue—which characteristics—began to increase in prominence. Today, it eclipses the first as the key determinant of naturalization. Despite Congress's steadily increasing interest in individual characteristics, we will demonstrate that qualifications for U.S. citizenship have been quite minimal throughout U.S. history. Thus, for the categories of immigrants eligible for U.S. citizenship, the nation has always been quite willing to welcome as citizens those individuals it has admitted as immigrants (in the twentieth century, those admitted as permanent resident immigrants).

Over the next several pages, we review the statutory history of U.S. naturalization law. We summarize this history in Table 3.2.

TABLE 3.2   Major Naturalization Laws Determining Who Can Immigrate and
What Standards They Must Meet, 1790–1997

Categories of Immigrants Eligible for and Excluded from U.S. Citizenship

Year	Category of Immigrant
1790	Free white persons (men) eligible
1798	Nationals of countries with which the United States is at war excluded from naturalization (repealed 1802)
1868	Citizenship extended to children born in the United States, regardless of the immigration status of the parent
1870	Aliens of African nativity eligible
1882	Chinese excluded from naturalization (other Asian nationalities also barred over next 40 years)
1906	Anarchists and polygamists excluded from naturalization
1912	Deserters and immigrants who left the United States to avoid the draft excluded from naturalization
1922	Women, regardless of marital status or citizenship status of husband, eligible
1943	Chinese eligible
1950	Communists or those who teach that the U.S. government should be overthrown excluded from citizenship
1952	Naturalization extended to all races

Characteristics or Abilities Required of Immigrants Seeking Naturalization

Year	Characteristic or Ability Required
1790	Resident in United States for two years; Good moral character; Willingness to take an oath or affirmation to support the Constitution
1795	Resident in the United States for five years; Willingness to renounce former allegiance; File a declaration of intention to naturalize three years before naturalization
1798	Resident in the United States for fourteen years; File the declaration of intention with the Attorney General
1802	Standards returned to 1795 law
1906	Speaking knowledge of English; State an intention to reside permanently in the United States; Provide two witnesses to five-year residence and good moral character
1950	Reading and writing knowledge of English; Knowledge and understanding of the fundamentals and principles of the forms of American government

Note: Congress has passed naturalization legislation since 1952. Relative to the legislation mentioned here, however, these recent laws have been primarily procedural. The foundations of today's naturalization requirements can be found in these pre-1952 laws.

Establishing the Foundations for U.S. Immigration Law

In one of its first acts, the first Congress established the framework for U.S. naturalization. The law addressed both the question of categories and individual qualifications. Congress extended the privilege of naturalization to all "free white persons." Among white immigrants, individuals had to have resided in the United
States for two years and in the state of application for one year. Aside from these
length of residence requirements, the first citizenship law required that applicants
be of "good character" and, upon award of citizenship, take an oath or affirmation
to support the Constitution. Children of the newly naturalized themselves became citizens through the parent's application (1 *Statutes at Large* 103, enacted
March 26, 1790). Although not stated explicitly in the law, the privilege of applying for citizenship was limited to men. The citizenship status of immigrant
women followed those of their husbands. In sum, the first naturalization law demanded little of individual applicants and thus encouraged naturalization among
the "free white persons" (men and their families).

Although simple in many ways, the outline established in this first citizenship law
offers a skeleton for subsequent amendments. It defined an eligible class of immigrants and established individual qualifications for their admission as citizens.

The first amendment to U.S. naturalization law came just five years later. In
1795, Congress extended the minimum period of U.S. residence to five years and
added two requirements. In addition to swearing allegiance to the Constitution,
new applicants had to renounce their former allegiance by name (1 *Statutes at
Large* 414, enacted January 29, 1795). In other words, an immigrant from England
had to renounce allegiance to the king of England. Aliens also had to renounce
hereditary titles to nobility, a requirement that remains today as a question on the
naturalization application.

Congress amended naturalization law once more in the eighteenth century. In
1798, it extended the period of residence required for naturalization to fourteen
years. This change was part of the anti-immigrant fervor of the Alien and Sedition
Acts. As part of its efforts to limit access to U.S. citizenship, Congress excluded
from eligibility citizens of countries with which the United States was at war.
Congress also attempted to centralize control over naturalization. The law required clerks of the local courts that administered naturalization to send the sec-
retary of state the names and applications of immigrants stating an intention to
become citizens (1 *Statutes at Large* 566, enacted June 18, 1798).

By 1802, national concern about the loyalty of immigrants had declined, and
Congress returned naturalization requirements to those established in 1795. The
requirement of five years of residence prior to naturalization enacted in 1802 has

not been changed since (2 *Statutes at Large* 153, enacted April 14, 1802). The brief effort to centralize control over naturalization also disappeared. For the next century, local officials applied the loose federal guidelines and determined who could join the polity.

Naturalization Law in the Nineteenth Century: Few Requirements, Slow Expansion of Eligibility

After these several changes in the nation's first decade, Congress largely ignored naturalization through the nineteenth century. The five-year length of residence requirement, good character, the oath or affirmation of loyalty to the Constitution, the renunciation of former allegiance, and the declaration of intention prior to the application remained the only barriers for immigrants seeking citizenship.

Congress did, however, return several times in the nineteenth century to reconfigure the categories of immigrants eligible to naturalize. Each was incidental to other broader changes in public policy. In 1870, Congress extended naturalization eligibility to aliens of African nativity (16 *Statutes at Law* 254, enacted July 14, 1870). This change initially applied to very few people, mostly to Afro-Caribbeans who had little ability or incentive to migrate prior to 1865. This was not the beginning of the liberalization of U.S. naturalization law. Instead, it is part of the **Radical Republican** efforts to legislate equal rights for blacks in one of the few policy areas controlled exclusively by the federal government. At a symbolic level, however, this change cannot be dismissed; it was the first time that naturalization extended beyond the 1790 standard of "free white persons."

Congressional action did not extend to all nonwhites, however. In 1882, among other provisions, the **Chinese Exclusion Act** barred the Chinese from naturalization (22 *Statutes at Large* 58, enacted May 6, 1882). The primary goal of this provision was to bar new Chinese immigration. In this, the law largely succeeded. It did not, however, prevent having any U.S. citizens of Chinese ancestry; the children of pre-1882 Chinese immigrants acquired U.S. citizenship at birth. Without new immigration, then, naturalization became irrelevant. Symbolically, however, the naturalization provisions of the Chinese Exclusion Act reinforced the statement of unwelcome found in the ban on Chinese immigration. Over the next forty years, Congress and the courts extended the prohibition on naturalization to other Asians, including nationals of India and other West Asians.

Perhaps unintentionally, Congress seemed to settle a major naturalization issue just after the Civil War. This concerned whether the U.S.-born children of noncitizens would become U.S. citizens or whether they would be treated as citizens of their parents' countries and, hence, need to naturalize to become U.S. citizens.

The **Fourteenth Amendment** to the Constitution granted immigrants' children citizenship based on their birth. Article 1 provides:

> All persons born or naturalized in the United States, and subject to the jurisdiction thereof, are citizens of the United States and of the State wherein they reside. No State shall make or enforce any law which shall abridge the privileges or immunities of citizens of the United States; nor shall any State deprive any person of life, liberty, or property, without due process of law; nor deny any person within its jurisdiction the equal protection of the laws.

When Congress proposed this amendment and the states ratified it, the citizenship status of the children of immigrants was not at issue. Instead, Congress sought to mandate the citizenship and equal protection rights of the recently freed slaves.[1] With the Fourteenth Amendment, however, Congress settled a conflict between the states. Some states had granted children born in the United States citizenship and others had not (Schuck and Smith 1985). Because there was no centralized control over the implementation of naturalization, these discrepancies between state decisions about who was a citizen went unaddressed until the passage of the Fourteenth Amendment.

The constitutional guarantee of *jus solis*, or birthright citizenship, created little debate at the time. There were relatively few immigrants, and their eventual movement into U.S. citizenship was assumed. More important, as we indicated in Chapter 2, there was no notion of undocumented immigration in this era. Only later did the status of immigrant children become a topic of congressional and popular concern. In a sense, however, Congress's action in this area is representative of its approach to naturalization in the nineteenth century. It was a topic of little concern that was addressed indirectly when it was addressed at all. For most immigrants in this era, requirements remained few, and the door to U.S. citizenship stayed wide open.

Naturalization in the Twentieth Century: Expanding Eligibility and Increasing Requirements

The steady expansion of immigration after the Civil War raised concerns about naturalization as well as immigration. This concern manifested itself in an increase in the requirements for those immigrants seeking to become U.S. citizens. Ending over a century without new individual-level naturalization requirements, Congress mandated in 1906 that citizenship applicants must have a speaking knowledge of English, state an intention to reside permanently in the United States, and provide two "credible" U.S. citizen witnesses who would provide affidavits stating that the naturalization applicant was of good moral character and had resided in the United States for five years (34 *Statutes at Large* 596, enacted June 29, 1906).

Congress also addressed the classes of immigrants eligible for naturalization. Excluded were anarchists and polygamists. Congress also enacted a series of procedural reforms in the administration of naturalization that we will discuss later in this chapter.

In sheer volume, the 1906 legislation was Congress's most extensive effort to date regarding naturalization. More important, perhaps, the English-speaking knowledge and the procedural reforms presaged Congress's approach to naturalization during the rest of the twentieth century. Since then, it has slowly expanded knowledge requirements for individuals seeking to naturalize and has tried—unsuccessfully, as we will indicate—to standardize the procedures for reviewing applicants and for granting naturalization. The exclusion of polygamists and anarchists also began a pattern of statutory exclusions of small categories of immigrants with beliefs or behaviors outside the mainstream of American society. In 1912, Congress excluded deserters or immigrants who left the United States to avoid the draft (37 *Statutes at Large* 356, enacted August 12, 1912).

The 1920s saw repeated efforts to streamline and eliminate inconsistencies in naturalization law. In contrast to the narrowing that was occurring in immigration policy, this period may be seen as one of steady liberalization in naturalization policy. The most notable of these changes reversed sexist aspects of naturalization law. Beginning in 1922, women (whether married or single) could apply for and be naturalized on their own (42 *Statutes at Large* 1021–1022, enacted September 22, 1922). This ended the previous practice that provided that foreign-born women were naturalized upon marriage to a U.S. citizen or upon the naturalization of their husband. Also, after 1922, female U.S. citizens no longer lost their citizenship upon marriage to a foreign male.

After the late 1920s, Congress did not revisit naturalization law until wartime pressures forced an acknowledgment that the provisions of the Chinese Exclusion Act were incompatible with wartime alliances. Thus, in 1943 Congress repealed the Chinese Exclusion Act and added Chinese to the populations eligible to immigrate and naturalize (57 *Statutes at Large* 600, enacted December 17, 1943). Then, in 1952 Congress extended access to naturalization to all Asians and explicitly to all races (66 *Statutes at Large* 163, enacted June 27, 1952). Although there were few immigrant Chinese and other Asians to take advantage of these liberalized naturalization provisions at first, this change is of great symbolic importance. It represents the elimination of the final national-origin, racial, or ethnic group excluded from access to U.S. citizenship (some groups united by belief or behavior continued to face exclusion).

ILLUSTRATION 3.1   Oath of Allegiance for Newly Naturalizing Citizens

I hereby declare, on oath, that I absolutely and entirely renounce and abjure all allegiance and fidelity to support any foreign prince, potentate, state or sovereignty, of whom or which I have heretofore been a subject or citizen; that I will support and defend the Constitution and laws of the United States of America against all enemies, foreign and domestic; that I will bear true faith and allegiance to the same; that I will bear arms on behalf of the United States when required by the law; that I will provide non-combatant service in the armed forces of the United States when required by the law; that I will perform work of national importance under civilian direction when required by law; and that I take this obligation freely without any mental reservation or purpose of evasion; so help me God.

While Congress was expanding the categories of immigrants eligible for U.S. citizenship, it was adding to the requirements with which immigrants seeking citizenship had to comply. Beginning in 1950, naturalization applicants had to demonstrate a knowledge and understanding of the fundamentals of the history and principles of the forms of the American government (64 *Statutes at Large* 1024, enacted September 23, 1950). Congress also expanded the language requirements enacted in 1906. Henceforth, applicants had to read, write, and speak "words in ordinary usage in the English language." This language requirement was not designed to be onerous for the applicant. Congress exempted applicants over fifty years old who had been residing in the United States for more than twenty years. Further, the law stated that the requirement was met if "applicant[s] can read or write simple words and phrases . . . and that no extraordinary or unreasonable conditions shall be imposed upon the applicant."

The 1950 law also created more classes of immigrants ineligible for naturalization based on beliefs. Joining polygamists, anarchists, and draft evaders were members of Communist organizations and those who advocated or taught that the U.S. government should be overthrown. The changes are virtually the last legislative efforts to define who is eligible for naturalization and what skills they must have.

Thus, today, the first policy question is largely resolved—no group is excluded on social, ethnic, or religious grounds. Instead, any immigrant who has resided in the United States for five years, is of good moral character, is willing to renounce loyalty to the country of origin, and is willing to swear (or affirm) loyalty to the Constitution and laws of the United States is eligible to become a U.S. citizen (see Illustration 3.1). These requirements date from the beginning of the republic. Few immigrants who meet these standards can be denied. Self-admitted polygamists, anarchists, Communists, and those who served in the Nazi regime are not eligible for U.S. citizenship. Also excluded from citizenship are immigrants who have committed certain crimes (felonies or multiple misdemeanors while permanent

Doonesbury

ILLUSTRATION 3.2   Doonesbury on Civic Knowledge Gained Through Naturalization. *Doonesbury* © 1996, 1997 G. B Trudeau. Reprinted by permission of *Universal Press Syndicate*. All rights reserved.

residents) and those who have been a public charge in the five years preceding the application for naturalization.

The second policy question—what traits the successful citizenship applicant should have—is not as settled as the first. Throughout this century, Congress has steadily increased the range of knowledge an applicant must have, and it may do so again in the future. Applicants must read, write, and speak English (with some exceptions for elderly immigrants who have lived in the United States for long periods). Also, they must demonstrate a knowledge and understanding of the fundamentals of U.S. history and the principles of U.S. government (see Illustration 3.2).

Who Should Administer the Award of Citizenship?

For its first century, U.S. naturalization policy was characterized by local administration. States and localities implemented the minimal federal standards and decided who could join the polity. As has been suggested, the federal laws that these local governments administered were more concerned with the question of what types of people were eligible for U.S. citizenship than with the skills and knowledge that individual immigrants possessed. The nature of local administration, however, was that whatever federal standards did exist were only loosely administered.

Beginning in the first decade of this century, the federal government centralized administration of the naturalization program. As we will indicate, this centralization eliminated the excesses created by local administration, but it created a system that has continued to be characterized by inconsistent administration. This inconsistency adds to the confusion that many applicants feel about how to proceed with their desires to naturalize as U.S. citizens. The failure to assure standardized administration reflects a problem in the delivery of many governmental services. These questions notwithstanding, however, this discussion of who should administer naturalization and what its result should be reinforces the findings of the previous section, specifically that the United States has designed a relatively inclusive system of naturalization that offers the prospect of membership to those categories of legal immigrants being welcomed.

Local Administration, 1790–1907

The Alien and Sedition Acts identified a problem that was to plague the administration of naturalization for the next century. The local governments that administered naturalization had virtual carte blanche. They evaluated whether naturalization applicants met the minimal federal standards, and then, assuming they determined that the applicant did, they provided documentation to demonstrate that the immigrant was a U.S. citizen. By contemporary standards, the Alien and Sedition Act's mandate that jurisdictions awarding naturalization provide the attorney general with the names of applicants so that the federal government could evaluate whether they were subjects of an enemy sovereign may seem minimal. Yet even that requirement fell in 1802, and federal review of individuals seeking naturalization was not to be resurrected for over one hundred years. The legacy of local administration remains today. As there was no reporting requirement, we have no idea how many immigrants earned U.S. citizenship through naturalization prior to 1907, and it is virtually impossible to determine if a specific immigrant naturalized in this era.

The excesses of local administration have been well documented. Urban machines relied on the lax federal administration to build their cadre of supporters. At the extreme, some immigrants were naturalized on the day of their arrival in the United States in open violation of the statutory requirement of a previous five-year residence in the United States. Before a particularly crucial election, New York's Tammany Hall machine printed 105,000 blank naturalization applications and 69,000 certificates of naturalization. "Immigrants fresh off the boat, were given red tickets, allowing them to get their citizenship papers free. Tammany paid the required court fees and provided false witnesses to testify that the immigrants had been in the country for the necessary five years" (Erie 1988:51).

What has been less documented is the impact outside of the urban machines. Without federal regulation, local governments could use their power to limit or facilitate access to naturalization. In the absence of extensive historical investigation, we can only speculate that both of these practices occurred. Many state and local governments in the late nineteenth and early twentieth centuries saw immigration as a rich pool for populating empty territory (these were the same governments that recruited immigrants in Europe and at ports of entry). Voting rights were extended to noncitizens, for example, explicitly to attract residents to states and territories needing people (Rosberg 1977).

In other areas, officials with nativistic impulses used local discretion to exclude from successful naturalization some immigrants who were otherwise statutorily eligible. Texas offers such an example. At the turn of the century, it was home to many immigrants and had large German, Czech, and French populations that had little difficulty in naturalizing. One nationality, however, faced difficulty—Mexicans. Whereas one notable case—*In re Rodríguez* (District Court for the Western District of Texas, May 3, 1897)—established a precedent assuring Mexican nationals of the right to naturalize, local authorities discouraged and intimidated Mexicans seeking to avail themselves of this right. In *Rodríguez*, the federal court naturalized Rodríguez based on Congress's granting of citizenship to the former subjects of Mexico in the Treaty of Guadalupe Hidalgo. The judge reasoned that the treaty guaranteed Mexicans the right of U.S. citizenship and that since that right was only available to white people, Mexicans, then, must be white. Texas, nevertheless, remained inhospitable to the citizenship rights of Mexicans for many years to come, while welcoming many other nationalities. Thus, local governments, often the same local government, facilitated naturalization for some and hindered it for others. Such contradictory patterns could coexist before centralized naturalization administration.

Although more research needs to be done on the treatment of citizenship applicants outside of the Eastern cities, the available data do indicate that many naturalized in this era. Despite the potential for local abuse and the exclusion of immigrants from citizenship, the pattern seems to have been the opposite: the use of local discretion to facilitate naturalization.

National Administration, 1907 to the 1990s

Congress became concerned that political machines naturalized ineligible immigrants. To address these concerns, President Theodore Roosevelt appointed an interagency commission in 1905. This commission designed the outline for the administration of today's naturalization program. Based on the commission's recommendations, Congress established the federal Bureau of Naturalization and enacted procedural reforms. Broadly, Congress's goals were to centralize administration and to assure that applicants met the statutory requirements for naturalization. In order to accomplish this goal, Congress took the power to grant naturalization away from local courts and the power to review applicants' credentials away from local officials. After 1907, only federal courts and designated state courts (in areas without sitting federal courts) could grant naturalization. Further, Congress required that investigations into applicants' eligibility, including the five-year period of residence and the English-language ability, be conducted by federal employees. The agency also created a single application form and a standard certificate of naturalization. Prior to this time localities had printed their own applications and had issued their own documents to prove naturalization. Finally, Congress standardized application fees nationwide. In 1907, it cost $4 to become a citizen of the United States (34 *Statutes at Large* 596, enacted June 29, 1906).

These reforms did not necessarily have the intended impact. In the more than eighty years that have elapsed since they were enacted, there has been a recurring pattern of inconsistency and a parallel concern that inconsistency may be impeding the immigrant's path to citizenship today.

Administrative inconsistencies under these reforms first appeared in the 1920s and 1930s. Several courts awarding naturalization interpreted the statutory requirement that applicants be "attached to" the principles of the Constitution as meaning that these courts should require a reading knowledge of English. Other courts mandated that applicants demonstrate a knowledge of civics, years before Congress mandated such knowledge.

Congress became sufficiently concerned about this variation in administration to appoint another investigatory commission to examine inconsistencies in the administration of naturalization. The result was legislation that further centralized the program's administration. Beginning in 1933, the newly consolidated Immigration and Naturalization Service received authority to recommend applicants for award or denial by the courts. In 1940, Congress transferred the INS from the Labor Department to the Justice Department (U.S. Senate 1980:41–42). Subsequently, courts largely came to accept the INS recommendations and tended to limit their involvement to applicants who sought judicial review after having been recommended for denial by the INS.

Variation in naturalization administration remains a problem plaguing the INS today. Applicants face a confusing bureaucracy that discourages many from pursuing their quest for U.S. citizenship. Of the immigrants who do pursue their application for naturalization, many face a confusing bureaucratic environment that does not treat applicants evenhandedly.

Recent studies have shown that many immigrants who had applied for naturalization never had their petitions submitted to the courts. The INS, acting on its own authority, used its power to review applications to encourage as many as one-fourth of applicants not to pursue their applications (North 1985). This rate of administrative denial far exceeds the judicial denial rate of between 2 and 4 percent (U.S. Immigration and Naturalization Service 1992, table 41).

Congressional concern over the wide use of administrative denials led to the mandate of a special review. Under the direction of the Senate Appropriations Committee, the INS evaluated administrative denial and reapplication rates in its larger offices (NALEO 1988, 1991). The results of this analysis validated congressional concerns and demonstrated the continuing problem of decentralization in the naturalization program. These studies found that administrative denials are used at vastly different levels by different INS offices and that they affect some nationalities more than others, with naturalization applicants from Mexico, Central and South America, and Africa more likely than immigrants from other regions of the world to experience administrative denials. Administrative denial rates in this study varied markedly among INS district offices. At one extreme, just 3.1 percent of Denver applicants faced administrative denial. In Miami, by contrast, 27.2 percent faced the same result.

The impact of this bureaucratic inconsistency on immigrants seeking to naturalize has only recently begun to be studied. To date, these studies have only examined Latino immigrants. As many as one-half the Latinos who initiate the application for naturalization fail to naturalize (Pachon and DeSipio 1994:chap. 7). Although some of this loss is undoubtedly a function of an individual's loss of interest, a great deal of it results from the administrative complexity of the process.

Congress's latest efforts at reform have done little to remedy the situation and, in fact, may have further entrenched INS decentralization. Responding to ongoing concerns about delays in processing citizenship applications, Congress in 1990 granted the INS the authority to award naturalization without judicial review. For successful applicants, this speeds the process by giving applicants the option of not waiting for a judge to administer the naturalization oath. Unsuccessful applicants continued to have recourse to the courts for judicial review. The review, however, was de novo, or without the benefit of the record of the INS application. This is a much more difficult process than the former procedure and lessens the likelihood that applicants facing INS denial will seek a court hearing. Thus, though the new procedure addressed one problem—administrative delays—it may well have worsened the problem of inconsistency.

The new INS jurisdiction has also increased the number of applicants whose applications are formally denied. The INS can now deny applications that it previously did not forward to the courts. In the 1980s—the decade before the INS received authority to award naturalization—slightly less than 2 percent of applications resulted in denials. In the 1990s, this rate surged to nearly 9 percent.

In sum, although Congress has steadily centralized the administration—first at the federal level and then in one agency, the Immigration and Naturalization Service—it has not been able to create a program that presents a common face to applicants across the country. In the next section, we look at who naturalizes and who does not. This examination of individual characteristics will expand upon our discussion of the administration of naturalization, allowing us to assess whether immigrants want to become citizens and what impedes those who do from naturalizing.

Who Naturalizes and Who Does Not?

So far in this chapter, we have examined the first dilemma in naturalization: Whom should the nation offer citizenship to? These discussions suggest that, for the most part, formal naturalization requirements have remained few and that despite administrative inconsistencies, many immigrants who seek to naturalize are able to make the transition to U.S. citizenship. These discussions have been quite general and have generally not differentiated among immigrants seeking citizenship. In this section, we will examine how different national-origin groups and various classes of immigrants engage the naturalization process.

Attachment to the United States and Interest in Naturalization

Throughout this discussion, there has been a largely unstated assumption that immigrants, particularly those with the five-year residency necessary to naturalize, want to stay in the United States and are interested in naturalization. This assumption defies a counterhypothesis appearing in many studies of U.S. immigration stating that many immigrants want to return to the sending country and stay in the United States only to earn capital to take home; this hypothesis, then, states that many immigrants are **sojourners** instead of settlers and future citizens.

We believe that the evidence refutes the sojourner view of immigrants. Although the question of the permanence of immigration has only been examined empirically in a few studies, the evidence is strong that immigrants intend to stay in the United States and want to naturalize.

The most conclusive of these studies is the National Latino Immigrant Survey. It finds that both in terms of attitudes and behaviors, Latino immigrants plan to stay in the United States and desire citizenship. At the simplest level, almost all Latino permanent resident immigrants with the five years of residence necessary to naturalize plan to reside in the United States for the rest of their lives. Even though the majority are not U.S. citizens, strong pluralities (approximately 40 percent) identify more with the United States than with their countries of origin. Two-thirds believe that it is very important to become a U.S. citizen, and an equal number have done something concrete to initiate the naturalization process, such as taking classes to prepare for the exam or obtaining the naturalization application (Pachon and DeSipio 1994). These immigrants clearly want to become part of American society. Subsequent studies of Latino immigrant populations reinforce these findings.

There are no comparable studies of attitudes about life in the United States or naturalization among immigrants from other parts of the world. In our judgment, the weight of the attachment to the United States among Latino immigrants strongly refutes sojourner notions of immigration. Instead, permanent resident immigrants are here to stay, and they desire political inclusion through naturalization. Despite this attachment, we find that the immigrant propensity to naturalize varies.

Propensity to Naturalize by National Origin

When academics and policymakers first examined naturalization, they asked a relatively simple question: Are some nationalities or types of immigrants more likely to naturalize than others? Although the question is simple, its answer potentially raises a problem for the polity. If the country were to admit large numbers of immigrants who had no interest in naturalization, it could create a pool of politically disengaged residents. These politically disengaged immigrants could become resentful of the decisions made for them by citizens. In a more extreme case, the admission of immigrants who oppose the politics of the host country and remain loyal to their sending country could come to act as a fifth column for the interests of their homeland. Should the sending country have designs on the receiving country's territory, this immigration could fundamentally challenge national sovereignty. Although there has been almost no evidence that the United States has faced politically destabilizing challenges from immigrants, policymakers and voters have feared this outcome at various points in U.S. history. As a result, the simple question of who is likely to naturalize and who is not has taken on serious implications.

Concerns about the loyalty of immigrants fueled two political crises in the nation's early years. The Alien and Sedition Acts resulted from both nationalistic and partisan fears. The governing Federalists feared not only that the loyalties of immigrants might drag the United States into the Napoleonic Wars but also that once they were naturalized, many of these immigrants might vote for the opposition. As a result, the naturalization law was changed to lengthen the necessary period of residence prior to naturalization and to test the loyalty of naturalization applicants. With the election of the Jeffersonians in the 1800 elections (in part based on the votes of naturalized citizens for Jefferson), the Alien and Sedition

Acts were quickly repealed. The next burst of anti-immigrant fervor followed the first great expansion in immigration in the late 1840s and 1850s. The American or Know-Nothing Party unsuccessfully called for the statutory period of residence for naturalization to increase to twenty-one years and for prohibiting naturalized citizens from holding public office. Each of these demands spoke to twin fears that have characterized periods of anti-immigrant fervor in the United States. First was the concern that the immigrants of the era were not Americanizing and that they could destabilize the polity. Second was a fear that they would be able to use the democratic process to supplant the political power of U.S.-born citizens and change the polity.

The first major national public policy debate about naturalization in this century had at its root a concern about different propensities to naturalize. As we suggested in Chapter 2, the effort to restrict immigration in the early decades of this century sought to reduce severely overall levels of immigration. Those few who would be allowed to immigrate would come from the countries that had provided the bulk of immigrants prior to 1880. The justification for this policy was research that demonstrated that immigrants from the areas that had provided immigrants prior to 1880—mostly Northern and Western Europe—had much higher naturalization rates than those who came from the countries that had provided most of the immigrants after 1880, that is, mostly Southern and Eastern European countries. This finding, based on the results of a study by a presidential commission, offered the intellectual justification for making American immigration law more restrictive and using immigration to reduce cultural conflict.

The finding was not so much wrong as incomplete. Even by the more limited analytical standards of the turn of the century, the Immigration Commission's approach was sloppy. It created a naturalization rate for each country of origin by examining the percentage of the total number of immigrants who had naturalized. This *raw* naturalization rate tells little. It compares nations that sent the majority of their emigrants in the 1870s with those that sent the majority of their emigrants in the few years immediately before the Immigration Commission conducted its study. Subsequent analysis that compared immigrants with similar lengths of residence found that there were few nationality-based variations in rate of naturalization (Gavit 1971 [1922]; Guest 1980). Although they enriched academics' knowledge of the naturalization process, these post–Immigration Commission findings came too late to change policy. As we mentioned in Chapter 2, U.S. immigration policy between 1922 and 1965 favored immigrants from Northern and Western European countries.

The lesson of this early examination of propensity to naturalize should not be lost on today's scholars. Examine similarly situated immigrants and do not expect just one characteristic—in this case, country of origin—to explain why some immigrants naturalize and others do not.

An examination of the largest immigrant-sending countries today would offer a similarly distorted picture. Table 3.3, for example, presents two measures of raw naturalization rates—those for all immigrants and those for immigrants who arrived in 1980 or later. In both cases, it reports on the share of immigrants who had naturalized by 1990. Among all foreign-born people counted in the 1990 census, it would appear that Europeans are the most likely to naturalize. Almost two-thirds of European immigrants (64.7 percent) had naturalized. Rates for other regions sending large numbers of immigrants to the United States—Asia, North America, and South America—are 40.8, 29.3, and 30.8 percent, respectively. Italians had the highest naturalization rate (75.8 percent) and Salvadorans had the lowest (15.4 percent) among the countries with the largest number of immigrants in the United States.

These data are distorted, though, because they reflect vastly different immigration histories. Foreign-born people in the United States who trace their ancestry to Europe are much more likely to have been in the United States for many years. More than 90 percent of Italians, for example, arrived prior to 1980. Three-fourths of Salvadorans, however, arrived in 1980 or after. Further, many of the Salvadorans arrived in the United States under immigration statuses that do not allow for naturalization.

Table 3.3 also examines raw naturalization rates for immigrants who arrived in 1980 or after who had naturalized by 1990 (many of these immigrants are ineligible to naturalize). These data offer a different picture of propensity to naturalize by national and regional origin. Among these recent immigrants, immigrants from Asia were the most likely to have naturalized (17.4 percent) and Central Americans the least likely (9.8 percent). Several of the national-origin groups had raw naturalization rates of less than 10 percent (Japan, United Kingdom, and Canada). Raw rates such as these, whether among all immigrants or recent immigrants, include many who are ineligible (permanent resident immigrants who arrived within the last five years, the undocumented, and others ineligible to naturalize).

Another strategy for assessing regions or nationalities and the propensity to naturalize is to follow a specific cohort of immigrants. Table 3.4 examines permanent resident immigrants who had naturalized by 1992. Among 1977 immigrants, Asians are joined by Africans as the most rapid naturalizers (56.2 percent and 53.9 percent, respectively). Europeans, North Americans, and the few immigrants from Oceania are the slowest (less than 30 percent). Among 1977 immigrants from specific countries, Filipinos had the highest rate of naturalization (61.3 percent) and Canadians the lowest (12.9 percent).

TABLE 3.3   Naturalization Rates for Regions and Countries of Origin with 250,000 or More Immigrants, 1990

Region and Country	Foreign-Born 1990	Raw Naturalization Rate (%)	Naturalization Rate (%) (among 1980 and later immigrants)
Europe	4,016,678	64.7	13.6
Germany	711,829	71.9	12.0
Italy	580,592	75.8	20.5
Poland	388,328	62.4	17.5
United Kingdom	640,145	49.6	7.1
Soviet Union	333,725	58.9	16.9
Asia	4,979,037	40.8	17.4
China	529,837	44.1	15.7
India	450,406	34.9	13.4
Japan	290,128	28.2	3.2
Korea	568,397	40.6	14.9
Philippines	912,674	53.9	25.9
Vietnam	543,262	42.7	26.6
North America	8,124,257	29.3	12.5
Canada	744,830	54.1	7.7
Mexico	4,298,014	22.6	12.7
Caribbean	1,938,348	39.7	15.1
Cuba	736,971	51.0	14.8
Dominican Rep.	347,858	27.6	14.0
Jamaica	334,140	38.4	17.2
Central America	1,133,978	20.7	9.8
El Salvador	465,433	15.4	10.1
South America	1,037,497	30.8	11.7
Colombia	286,124	29.0	11.2
Africa	363,819	34.1	15.4
Oceania	104,145	34.0	12.6
Total	19,767,316	40.5	14.4

Note: The countries of origin listed are those with 250,000 or more of their former nationals residing in the United States in 1990.

Source: U.S. Bureau of the Census, 1993b.

TABLE 3.4   Naturalization Rates for Regions and Countries Providing 5,000 Immigrants in 1977: Immigrants from 1977 Naturalized by 1992

Region and Country	Admitted 1977	Naturalizations Through 1992	Rate (%)
Europe	54,868	15,340	28.0
Greece	6,577	2,004	30.5
Italy	5,843	916	15.7
Portugal	6,964	1,622	23.3
United Kingdom	8,982	1,611	17.9
Asia	119,226	67,033	56.2
China	14,421	8,470	58.7
India	15,033	7,705	51.3
Korea	19,824	10,843	54.7
Philippines	31,686	19,415	61.3
Africa	7,713	4,161	53.9
Oceania	2,927	632	21.6
North America	142,313	42,240	29.7
Canada	9,000	1,161	12.9
Mexico	30,967	5,130	16.6
Cuba	57,023	20,522	36.0
Dominican Republic	8,955	1,939	21.7
Jamaica	7,896	3,065	38.8
South America	25,024	9,931	39.7
Colombia	6,138	2,214	36.1
All countries	352,071	139,337	39.6

Note: The INS does not collect data on immigrants who subsequently emigrate or who die. As a result, it is not possible to determine how many 1977 immigrants continued to reside in the United States in 1992.

Source: Immigration and Naturalization Service, 1994, table 58.

Although this method of measuring propensity to naturalize might seem more valid, it too has failings. First, naturalization rates vary significantly by year of immigration, so it is not possible to create a reliable picture of nationalities and propensities to naturalize from examination of a single year's immigrants. Second, the INS does not maintain data on the emigration and mortality of permanent residents. Thus, by 1992, many immigrants might have died or left the United States.

Only two studies (controlling for the impact of other factors discussed in the next section) examine the propensity of different nationalities to naturalize in a methodologically sophisticated manner. In a study of all 1971 immigrants, Guillermina Jasso and Mark Rosenzweig (1990) found that Mexicans were less likely than other national-origin groups to naturalize within ten years. DeSipio (1996) found that among Latinos, Mexicans were less likely than Cubans and Dominicans to naturalize. No comprehensive study of all nationalities and naturalization propensity exists to test these findings.

In sum, it is quite difficult to determine the propensity to naturalize. It is important to note that although some nationalities show consistently higher patterns of naturalization, all nationalities and regions demonstrate steadily increasing levels of naturalization over time. In the next section, we indicate some factors that help distinguish between nationalities with high naturalization rates and those with lower rates, or, more accurately, between those that naturalize quickly and those who do so more slowly.

Propensity to Naturalize by Denizen Characteristics

Beginning in 1936, new research began to examine a wide range of factors that might influence naturalization. These fit broadly into two categories—status and psychological characteristics. Status examines the impact of socioeconomic factors, such as income, education, and occupation, on the propensity to naturalize. Psychological characteristics include immigration and acculturation characteristics, such as reasons for immigration visa eligibility, English-language ability, and attachment to the United States. Despite the added complexity of this contemporary research, it is still not possible to say with certainty why one immigrant will naturalize and why another will not. Instead, we may speak of some factors that seem to influence the propensity to naturalize.

The most reliable predictor of the propensity to naturalize is time; that is, the longer immigrants are in the United States, the higher the chance that they will be U.S. citizens. Relatedly, older immigrants are more likely to have naturalized. This impact is felt over and above the effect of length of residence. These are the only two traits that consistently have a positive impact on naturalization. Other status factors that appear in some studies to positively predict naturalization include socioeconomic factors such as high median income, white-collar employment, professional status, high levels of education, home ownership, young children in the household, and being female or being married (Barkan and Khokolov 1980; Portes and Mozo 1985; Jasso and Rosenzweig 1990; Yang 1994; DeSipio 1996).

Studies have also identified psychological factors that are related to immigration and acculturation, including the following: emigration for political reasons, entrance as skilled laborers or refugees, origin in Asia or Africa, immigration from a country distant from the United States, and immigration from an English-speaking country (Portes and Mozo 1985; Jasso and Rosenzweig 1987, 1990; Yang 1994). The process of acculturation proves to be a positive predictor of naturalization in some studies, particularly such acculturation factors as the following: social identification as an American, roots in the United States (home ownership, children born in the United States, and immediate family in the United States), residence in areas with non-coethnics, positive attitude toward life in the United States, demystification of the naturalization process, increasing attachment to the United States, finding intermediaries to help with the naturalization application, and increasing proficiency with English (García 1981; Alvarez 1987; Portes and Curtis 1987; DeSipio 1996).

Why can we only discuss these factors as likely indicators of naturalization instead of more confidently stating their individual impacts? To begin with, there are no comprehensive studies of all immigrants from all nations of the world that can disaggregate immigrants eligible for naturalization or those who have naturalized. Instead, studies of all foreign-born individuals tend to rely on Bureau of the Census data that include undocumented immigrants and others ineligible to naturalize (Barkan and Khokolov 1980; Yang 1994). Data from the Immigration and Naturalization Service allow analysis of legal immigrants who have naturalized, but INS data do not include psychological variables.

This analytical imprecision will only be overcome through continued and more sophisticated study in the future. Since immigration continues at high rates and naturalization lags behind, we assume that more rigorous study will eventually be done. The cost of such comprehensive study, however, dictates that we will likely be relying on indicators such as those presented here for some time.

Naturalization in the United States: Entering the Third Century

With the rapid increase in immigration since 1965, naturalization is again a focus of interest among public policy makers and average citizens alike. The history of naturalization law and practice offers a guide to one possible outcome of this interest: relatively easy access to citizenship among these immigrants, administered somewhat erratically by the federal government, with some immigrants more likely to take advantage of this opportunity than others. Of course, the historical

patterns offer just one possible pattern. Whatever course the nation follows in responding to the need for immigrant political inclusion, it currently faces three
policy questions that will shape how the naturalization process interacts with immigrants in the coming years. These three policy questions all relate to the second
dilemma: On what terms should the United States admit immigrants to membership? The United States will have to define the appropriate benefits of citizenship
that distinguish citizens from noncitizens, the appropriate role of government in
promoting citizenship to eligible immigrants, and the citizenship status of the
children of immigrants born in the United States.

The Benefits of Citizenship

Despite its importance to the polity, the nation has never comprehensively examined the rights and benefits that should be unique to citizens (and denied to noncitizens). As we have suggested, when policymakers discuss naturalization, they focus
on procedural questions—what categories of immigrants should be excluded from
citizenship and who should administer the award of citizenship. Although the slowly
increasing standards for individual applicants may be viewed as a statement that we
as a people are demanding more of our voluntary citizens, Congress's explicit statement and the INS's practice of requiring little of citizenship applicants diminish the
value of these requirements as a measure of the meaning of citizenship.

Where then can we look for this meaning? One way would be to look at the differences in the rights and privileges of U.S. citizens and non-U.S. citizens. Between citizens and legal permanent resident aliens, these differences have traditionally been few, though they have recently increased dramatically. The gap is
much wider between citizens and permanent residents on the one hand, and undocumented immigrants on the other. Even the undocumented, however, have
significant rights in our society. More specifically, like citizens and permanent resident aliens, they enjoy basic constitutional rights and due process guarantees.

The differences that have traditionally distinguished the rights and privileges of
permanent residents and citizens relate to narrowly defined job rights and programmatic benefits for recent immigrants. In terms of employment, Congress
and many of the states exclude permanent residents from employment in most
federal, state, and local government jobs and in private sector jobs requiring security clearances. As public employment has traditionally been a means for educated immigrants to gain a foothold, these limitations on employment could be
seen as a serious impediment. In other sectors of the economy, however, permanent residents have equal access to employment.

Until recently, few federal benefit programs restricted eligibility to U.S. citizens.
Two exceptions were scholarships administered by the federal government and

access to full social security benefits upon retirement. The latter restriction only applied to permanent residents who retired abroad. Over the past fifteen years, the federal government enacted waiting periods, after which permanent resident immigrants became eligible for social welfare programs, particularly needs-based programs. These waiting periods lasted up to five years.

In 1996, Congress dramatically expanded the difference in programmatic eligibility between permanent residents and U.S. citizens. We discuss these changes and the justifications for them in greater detail in Chapter 4, but for now, suffice it to say that as a result of the 1996 Immigration and Welfare Reform Bills, newly arriving permanent residents have lost eligibility for major federal programs such as Supplemental Security Income (SSI) and food stamps and are subject to state determinations of eligibility (and the willingness of the state to pay the benefits) for Medicaid and Temporary Aid to Needy Families (TANF) (formerly Aid to Families with Dependent Children, or AFDC). In 1997, Congress restored permanent resident eligibility for SSI.

As important as these changes are, both for the lives of individual immigrants and for the broader question of the meaning of citizenship in the modern era, there was little debate in Congress about how these changes would affect immigrants and immigrant incorporation. Instead, in 1996 members of Congress saw an easy source of cuts in welfare spending that they thought would be less controversial and politically risky than other sources of funds (for example, Medicare spending). In 1997, in relatively flush economic times, they responded to pressure to restore SSI benefits. In neither case, however, were there discussions of how these changes would affect immigrant incorporation.

Although it is too early to analyze the impact of these changes, it is safe to say that Congress created a material incentive to naturalize that did not exist prior to 1996. Immigrants seeking to retain or establish eligibility for benefits may now naturalize, not for civic reasons but for more instrumental objectives. The vast increase in applications for naturalization that began in the early 1990s and continues today may, in fact, reflect immigrants seeking to protect themselves against future economic adversity (applicants who have regularly used these federal programs are ineligible to naturalize as they can be deemed public charges, so current beneficiaries are not naturalizing so they can retain their existing benefits).

The Government and Naturalization Promotion

Our discussion of who should administer naturalization gives rise to another important question: Is it the government's responsibility to promote naturalization? The history of the U.S. naturalization program offers no clear answer. Instead, there are several conflicting models for government involvement in citizenship promotion.

Prior to 1907, promoting citizenship, like administering naturalization, was conducted locally. In practice, this meant active encouragement in some areas and neglect in others. The political machines of the big cities offer an example of active encouragement. The presence of a machine, however, did not guarantee citizenship assistance and promotion. For example, Irish-led machines became more selective in their offers of assistance after non-Irish immigrants came to dominate the pool of the naturalization-eligible and elections became less competitive.

During the twentieth century, the federal government has been responsible for administering naturalization. Among these administrative responsibilities, promotion has until very recently not been very important. This approach to naturalization promotion is best summarized by E. B. Duarte, the INS's director of outreach: "The Immigration and Naturalization Service does not have a policy that identifies lawful permanent residents eligible for citizenship or that encourages them to apply for naturalization. . . . The reason is that naturalization is viewed as a voluntary act" (NALEO 1986:16).

According to Duarte, the INS only becomes involved once an immigrant (or a community-based organization) approaches it with an application or a request for assistance. This narrow role has allowed for certain educational activities. The INS is authorized to use a small share of naturalization fees to produce textbooks for use in citizenship education classes. The Department of Education allows federal adult education funds to be used by local school districts to offer citizenship classes. Traditionally, however, the INS has not promoted naturalization.

In the early 1990s, the Immigration and Naturalization Service's approach began to change this long-held practice of not promoting naturalization. Controversy surrounding these efforts may, however, reduce these initiatives in the future. In November 1993, INS Commissioner Doris Meissner announced that the INS would promote naturalization. This effort has included direct contact with immigrants and earmarking funds for community-based organizations to provide information to immigrants seeking citizenship (Pear 1993). These efforts took on a new intensity in late 1995 and 1996 with added commitments of agency resources and personnel. The INS called this program "Citizenship USA."

The incentives for this intensification were mixed. In part, they reflected a record number of unprocessed applications—as many as 1.5 million (beginning in 1993, the number of applications surged). Evidently, there were also political considerations, with the White House interested in processing as many of the applications as possible before the election. In its effort to review as many applications as possible, the INS approved applicants once it had waited for 120 days for FBI review of the applicant's fingerprints. This decision allowed the INS to process over 1 million naturalization applications in 1996, a record. It also spurred controversy when it became evident that as many as 5,000 new citizens with criminal records that should have barred their naturalization became U.S. citizens. In response, the INS has initiated denaturalization proceedings against the inappropriately naturalized and Congress and the Justice Department have initiated high-profile investigations of Citizenship USA. More important for the study of naturalization, though, the legacy of this failed effort to promote naturalization was a retreat from the new interest in promoting naturalization. It looked as though the INS would again process more than 1 million applications in 1997, but that now seems very unlikely.

Birthright Citizenship

The award of birthright citizenship after 1870 has had a profound impact on the way both immigrants and natives think about immigrants and naturalized citizens. Regardless of whether immigrant parents naturalize, their U.S.-born children receive U.S. citizenship.

Birthright citizenship is not the norm among other developed countries. Many nations do not extend citizenship to the native-born children of immigrants (or for that matter to the native-born children of native-born children of immigrants). German citizenship, for example, must derive either from a blood tie to a German citizen or from naturalization. Until recently, France and Australia automatically granted citizenship to the native-born children of immigrants. Concerns about the number and costs of immigrants prompted changes in 1993 and 1986, respectively, by both France and Australia. France, like Germany, now requires that citizenship derive from family ties or from naturalization (Brubaker 1992). Australia now requires that parents be citizens or legally resident in Australia for the child to be granted Australian citizenship. If the United States should seek to change provision of citizenship by birth, these recent changes in French and Australian policy offer two possible paths to follow.

Birthright citizenship has also generated controversy in the United States. Governor Pete Wilson of California and members of the Senate and the House of Representatives have proposed, at least rhetorically, that U.S.-born children of undocumented immigrants be denied citizenship.

Although it is not possible to unite the positions of all opponents to birthright citizenship into a single camp, the arguments they make are several. First, they have practical concerns about the impact of the current guarantees that relate to both the parent and the child. For the parent, they are concerned that the guarantee of citizenship for U.S.-born children stimulates undocumented migration among adults. Opponents also argue that undocumented parents believe that they are less likely to be deported if they have U.S.-born children. The second practical concern of opponents is the cost of birthright citizenship. States that receive large numbers of undocumented migrants provide social services such as education and health care based on the presence of these U.S.-born children. A simple, or perhaps simplistic, calculus suggests that if these children could be denied citizenship and, hence, services, states and localities would spend less.

Opponents of birthright citizenship also base their positions on philosophical and nationalistic concerns. They argue that nations must control their borders. Granting citizenship based on an illegal act (undocumented migration) extends membership in the society to those who have never been invited to join (the U.S.-born children of the undocumented migrant) and hence transfers decisions about membership to those who have no respect for U.S. law. They are concerned, then, that American society is losing control of its future destiny.

Supporters of birthright citizenship have not had to defend their positions as rigorously as the opponents. The seeming clarity of the constitutional language and the absence of any serious judicial challenges or legislative efforts to amend the Constitution have limited the need to fight to maintain its guarantees. The beginning of such a challenge, however, has formed the foundation of a defense. Again, this defense has both practical and philosophical dimensions. At a practical level, advocates of birthright citizenship do not want to create a permanent intergenerational pool of noncitizens in the nation. The elimination of birthright citizenship would mean that the children or grandchildren of immigrants would remain partially in and partially outside of the society. This partial exclusion could lead to the formation of an illegal, exploitable underclass among individuals who are stateless. Germany provides an example of this dilemma, with its two and three generations of Turkish immigrants and their children, who reside with the right to stay permanently but without access to German citizenship. These German-born children and grandchildren of immigrants have no ties to Turkey and could not easily be deported to a homeland they have never visited.

Advocates also raise a philosophical concern. The elimination of birthright citizenship punishes the child for the action of the parent. Thus, advocates deny that a qualitative difference exists at birth between the child of an undocumented immigrant and the child of a descendant of the first colonizers. In this case, they make a claim of equal protection before the law.

The opponents of birthright citizenship have seized the popular concern about the volume and composition of immigration to shift the debate about birthright citizenship from the academic sphere with the ultimate goal of changing either the wording or the interpretation of the Fourteenth Amendment. How are they setting out to accomplish this goal? Most directly, members of Congress have introduced constitutional amendments to delete references to "born in the United States" from the qualifications for citizenship. These proposed amendments have met with little success.

The failure of the direct approach has generated a concerted effort to engage the courts in the debate. To date, there has been no judicial interpretation of the meaning of the clause "and subject to the jurisdiction thereof" in the Fourteenth Amendment. Birthright citizenship opponents see this clause as the Achilles' heel of the provision. The opponents vary on whether they believe that all immigrants (permanent residents and the undocumented alike) or just undocumented immigrants are not "subject to the jurisdiction" of the U.S. government; they assert that this provision denies birthright citizenship to many who today are its beneficiaries. This effort to engage the courts in this debate has taken several forms. Members of Congress have introduced laws denying citizenship to the children of immigrants. Were they to pass, these laws would be challenged on constitutional grounds, forcing the issue into the courts. This challenge is also occurring at the state level. The constitutional challenges to Proposition 187 may involve birthright citizenship, as courts will be asked to evaluate equal protection claims of U.S. citizen children of undocumented immigrants.

Even if the courts sidestep this issue in these cases, proponents of Proposition 187 are reported to be developing an initiative to force a judicial challenge to the common interpretation of the Fourteenth Amendment. If this initiative is carefully phrased and passed by California voters, the courts may be forced to take on this issue. As we have suggested, the courts have not been involved in this debate to date, so the outcome is in question.

These efforts to challenge birthright citizenship may be for naught because the courts may affirm the status quo or sidestep the issue entirely. The underlying debate, nevertheless, is of fundamental importance. It seeks to define who is a member of the polity and how that privilege will be passed to the next generation. Although there is some ambiguity in the debate about whether it would affect the children of all immigrants or just those of the undocumented, it indicates a growing interest in narrowing access to U.S. citizenship.

Conclusion

Although occasionally the focus of public concern and even outright fear, naturalization has long been guaranteed to immigrants to the United States. Throughout its history, the United States has offered immigrants access to nearly full political incorporation. Formal requirements have remained few, and throughout much of the nation's history, enforcement of these requirements has remained lax. Although the polity was initially narrow in the categories of immigrants to whom citizenship was offered, the naturalization law has always reflected the immigration patterns of the day; thus there were few immigrants to the United States in any era who were ineligible to naturalize.

The surge in immigration that followed the 1965 amendments to the immigration law has again caused the nation to assess its openness to the political incorporation of the foreign-born. Although formal requirements remain few and eligibility is no longer restricted by nationality, varying propensities to naturalize (despite high levels of interest) and bureaucratic inconsistencies keep many immigrants in a semipermanent state of noncitizenship (denizenship).

This potentially poses a conundrum for the nation regarding both identity and practical concerns. In terms of identity, the state must decide whether it should encourage interested immigrants to naturalize. At a more practical level, the state must question whether the narrow difference in rights and responsibilities between citizens and noncitizens acts as a deterrent to naturalization. Further, the United States must assess whether it is healthy for a polity to have such a high share of its residents formally loyal to foreign sovereigns.

The significance of this conundrum is intensified for the polity for reasons that we discuss in greater depth in Chapter 4. Increasingly, some societal benefits are allocated based on a desire to redress past wrongs. Affirmative action benefits target the victims and descendants of those whom society has discriminated against. The categories of beneficiaries of these programs have increasingly become clouded by high rates of immigration. Programs initially designed to assist "minorities" now also benefit immigrants who share ethnicity with the original beneficiaries. Increasingly, then, as policymakers think about immigrant incorporation, they must consider the overlap between the basic issue of immigrant settlement policies discussed in this chapter and policies with quite different purposes. Thus, as the United States assesses settlement policies for today's immigrants, a new factor has been added to the debate that was not there for past generations of immigrants.

Notes

1. As our focus is naturalization, we are not concerned with blanket grants of citizenship such as that in the Fourteenth Amendment for African Americans. In several other cases, Congress provided citizenship to groups, usually in response to peoples in territories appended to the United States. These included former Mexican subjects in the Southwest in 1848, former Russian subjects in Alaska in 1867, native Hawaiians in 1900, Puerto Ricans in 1917 (after they lost their Spanish nationality in 1900), American Indians in 1924, Virgin Islanders in 1927, and Guamanians in 1950.

4

Immigrants and Natives: Rights, Responsibilities, and Interaction

So far, we have examined the legal and administrative aspects of immigration and naturalization. Clearly, however, the process of immigrant adaptation involves more than simply the questions of whom the nation will admit and the procedure by which they become citizens. Equally important is the legal relationship between immigrant and U.S.-born populations, an issue we examine in this chapter. This legal relationship is distinct from the formal process of incorporation through naturalization examined in Chapter 3. Here, we look at policy areas where the needs of immigrants may come into conflict with those of the U.S.-born and examine how the U.S. government resolves these conflicts.

We assess the process of immigrant-native adaptation in three ways. First, we examine what rights, privileges, and responsibilities noncitizens have in U.S. society so as to see what opportunities and restrictions immigrants face. Second, we discuss an emerging debate in the society over state government efforts to shape immigration policy by allocating different sets of state benefits to immigrants and natives. Finally, we look at how policies designed to assist other groups within U.S. society, particularly minority populations, affect immigrants.

These three discussions offer a portrait of the interactions structured by the state between immigrants and native populations. Throughout this discussion, we will indicate what resources are available to today's immigrants for settlement. By "settlement," we mean the governmental resources that are available to assist immigrants in making the transition from immigrant to full and equally participating member of the society. As we will show, many of the policies that benefit immigrants in the United States were not designed with immigrants in mind. Instead, Congress authored them for other populations, particularly U.S.-born minorities. As a result, these policies do not necessarily meet the needs of immigrants and may serve to shape the immigrant experience in a way that will lead to greater demand in the future for government programs to remedy past discrimination (what we call **remedial programs**).

Noncitizen Responsibilities

Noncitizens have many of the same responsibilities to the state as citizens. Noncitizens must obey the laws of the land and are subject to all forms of taxation, including taxes for the Social Security program (the Federal Insurance Contributions Act, or FICA). Noncitizen males must register for the draft and are then subject to the draft on an equal basis. Noncitizens may not serve on juries, but they are subject to the same criminal and civil law as citizens. In a sense, they can never be judged by a jury of their peers.

Noncitizens have also experienced responsibilities unknown to the citizen population. From 1940 through 1981, noncitizens had to report their address to the government annually (95 *Statutes at Large* 1611, enacted December 20, 1981). Immigration law restricts the amount of time permanent residents can spend outside of the country. Extended absences can result in the loss of resident status. Finally, immigration laws could be changed to alter the status of permanent residents. This danger, though slight, always places permanent residents at risk of losing any or all rights, privileges, and responsibilities.

Noncitizen Rights and Privileges

For the past sixty years up until the passage of the 1996 Welfare Reform Bill, few rights and privileges have been denied to permanent resident immigrants as the modern social welfare state has evolved. Many more rights and privileges, however, have been denied to the undocumented. The rights and privileges denied to immigrants can be understood as fitting broadly into three categories—electoral, employment/occupational, and programmatic. As we will suggest, the denials of programmatic benefit privileges are the ones being most actively debated in Congress and in state legislatures today.

Rights and privileges are often confused. We will use the term "rights" to refer to fundamental guarantees provided in the Constitution, such as voting. Although these rights can be reversed by legislatures, a reversal requires an amendment to the Constitution. "Privileges," however, refer to the statutory implementation of rights. For example, the Constitution guarantees equal protection under the law. Nonetheless, not all discrimination is unlawful. According to judicial rulings, legislatures can lawfully discriminate, depending upon the type of discrimination and what public interest is at stake. We examine two areas of public policy in which privileges are selectively denied to noncitizens. The partially denied privileges involve rights to nondiscrimination in employment and in the receipt of government benefits.

Electoral Rights

With few exceptions, noncitizens cannot participate in electoral politics. They are barred from voting in all federal and state elections and most local races. This pattern of exclusion extends equally to the documented and undocumented. A few jurisdictions—Cambridge, Massachusetts, and Takoma Park, Maryland, for example—grant the **franchise** to noncitizens in municipal elections. Other jurisdictions, most notably New York City, grant noncitizen parents the vote in local school board elections. Thus, although there are a few exceptions, the general rule is that noncitizens do not vote in U.S. elections.

This has not always been the case. As recently as the turn of the century, more than one-half of the states had granted long-term noncitizens the vote or had done so in the recent past (Rosberg 1977). The federal government had also permitted noncitizen voting in some of the territorial governments. These states and territories with noncitizen voting, primarily in the Midwest and West, were not necessarily acting out of a sense of altruism or to promote a rigorous conception of democracy. Instead, they saw the franchise as a lure for immigrants to settle in their states. As national support for immigration declined in the first decades of this century, the number of states granting the franchise to noncitizens also declined, ending with the removal of the franchise privilege in Arkansas in 1926.

The U.S. Constitution does not address this aspect of voting rights. Instead, it is the states that have the power to grant this privilege. Some state constitutions prohibit noncitizen voting outright, thus preventing localities from extending noncitizens the vote. Other constitutions, such as those in Massachusetts, New York, and Maryland, allow local jurisdictions to set their own voting rules for local elections.

Many immigrant advocates assert that extending the franchise to immigrants offers a valuable, largely untapped tool that would simultaneously empower immigrant communities and connect them further to American society. In their support for this proposition, they tap into the American creed—noting that immigrants pay taxes yet have no say in their representation. This claim of taxation without representation supplements a more practical argument. In the cities with immigrant concentrations, local officials have no electoral connection to the majority of their constituents. Thus, they may not represent the needs of these unfranchised constituents. By extending the franchise to noncitizens, then, jurisdictions could assure better representation, arguably the goal of democratic government. Within immigrant populations, the noncitizen vote would offer a tool for mobilization and might serve to maintain community cohesion.

Proposals to grant the franchise to noncitizens have not received extensive support beyond that of immigrant community leaders. As a result, there has been no coordinated opposition or single set of arguments shared by all who oppose the idea. The notion that links opposition to noncitizen voting is the idea that voting is a privilege that is reserved for citizens. Only citizens have the appropriate stake in the country or the government to make the sorts of decisions that would be in the nation's best interests. Although not articulated, this is the position of most jurisdictions nationally.

As few governments have seriously considered adopting noncitizen voting, there has been little analysis of its potential impact, whether on immigrant populations or on local, state, or national governments. Arguably, the impact of an energized noncitizen electorate could be great in cities such as Los Angeles, Houston, Miami, and Chicago, with their sizable noncitizen populations. If there were a close election in which the noncitizen population was cohesive and the citizen population divided, this impact could extend to statewide elections in immigrant-receiving states such as California, Texas, Florida, and New York. Although the likelihood of noncitizen influence in national politics would be remote even if noncitizens were to be granted the vote in all fifty states, it must be noted that the only "national" race—the campaign for the presidency—is in fact just fifty state races in which the winner takes all of the state's electoral votes. Thus, in a very close race that is determined by the votes of the larger states (most of which are immigrant-receiving states), an empowered noncitizen electorate could swing the election. The scenarios vary from the possible—influence in local elections—to the highly unlikely, that is, national or state-level influence.

Advocates of noncitizen voting have not been, and have not had to be, very specific about their proposals. It is not clear, for example, whether advocates of noncitizen voting seek to extend the right to all offices at all levels of government or just to local races. Nor has there been any discussion about when noncitizens should be eligible to vote should they be given the privilege. At the turn of the century, most states did not extend the franchise to immigrants until they had filed their "**first papers**"—a formal statement of intention to naturalize—after a minimum of three years of U.S. residence. Because of these changes in the structure of voting since the turn of the century, advocates of noncitizen voting cannot simply rely on the fact that it once existed. Instead, advocates need to specify what they are calling for and how this form of voting would interact with contemporary voting law and practice.

We think that regardless of one's philosophical attitudes toward noncitizen voting, in the contemporary political environment it has a serious flaw: Few noncitizens would use the right. Most noncitizens have the characteristics of those in the society who do not vote (de la Garza and DeSipio 1993). Immigrants are younger, less educated, and poorer than the average citizen. Regardless of race or ethnicity, young adults vote less than older adults; the poor vote less than the middle class or the rich; and the less educated vote less than the more educated. Noncitizens, thus, are like those in U.S. society who do not participate in electoral politics. In addition to these demographic factors that influence all potential electorates, many noncitizens face another barrier. Many do not speak English or speak it poorly. The Voting Rights Act (VRA) requires that registration and voting materials be available to Asians and Spanish speakers in their native languages in areas where their density or numbers are great (we discuss these requirements later in this chapter). Information about candidates, issues, and campaigns, however, is available primarily in English. Thus, noncitizens would not only face the demographic and structural barriers experienced by all potential voters but also linguistic barriers to information and, for non-Asians and non-Spanish speakers, to registration and voting materials.

These concerns about the utility of noncitizen voting are substantiated by observations of noncitizen participation in those few areas that today permit it. There is little evidence that noncitizens exercise their right in great numbers, even in local school council elections that presumably have direct importance to noncitizen parents. Thus, at the individual level, we believe that few noncitizens would take advantage of the franchise.

Two populations suffer if noncitizens do not receive the franchise—the undocumented and the permanent resident immigrants with less than five years of legal residence. The status of the undocumented is such that they will never be able to naturalize or vote. In the current political environment, it is unlikely that states or localities would consider extending them the franchise. At a more conceptual level, their status raises the question of what the franchise means. Is it a quid pro quo for paying taxes or for residing geographically within a nation's territory? Or is it an act of trust extended to those who have a long-term stake in the society? The way people answer these questions probably shapes their view on whether the franchise should be extended to the undocumented.

A more problematic dilemma relates to the rights of the recently arrived permanent resident. Although these new arrivals will attain citizenship eligibility and then voting eligibility in the future, the process takes five years. Further, they potentially have a long-term stake in the society, so their claim on the vote is stronger than that of undocumented immigrants. In our work, we have suggested that a case can be made for extending the franchise to permanent residents not yet eligible to naturalize that would be limited to the period before their statutory eligibility to apply for naturalization (de la Garza and DeSipio 1993). Although we believe that few would take advantage of this limited noncitizen voting, we think that those who were to vote regularly would be demonstrating the sort of good citizenship that the naturalization exam seeks to measure through its knowledge-based measure (history, civics, and English-language knowledge). For those immigrants who were to vote regularly during this five-year period of citizenship ineligibility, we would grant citizenship automatically upon application.

We disagree on the sorts of elections that short-term permanent residents should be eligible to vote in. Because of concerns about their ability to shape national policy, particularly policy toward their sending countries, de la Garza would extend this limited noncitizen voting only for state and local elections. DeSipio, however, fears the administrative burdens to local election officials of having to create two sets of voting lists and two ballots would allow permanent residents to vote in all elections during the first five years of residence. Again, it is important to note that neither of us thinks that many noncitizens would vote in large numbers under this proposal.

The question of the rights of noncitizens to electoral access raises fundamental questions about the link between the polity and its residents. Although noncitizens have largely been excluded from the franchise, there have been notable and long-term exceptions where they voted in all elections.

We conclude with the observation that the question of who should participate in U.S. politics has been an active topic of debate from the nation's first days and will likely never be finally resolved. Initially a privilege of white male citizen landholders, it slowly expanded to all white citizens, to women, to African Americans, and to those between the ages of eighteen and twenty. Each of these formal expansions of the electorate accompanied a new sense of who had a stake in what the nation did. Thus, the meaning of citizenship expanded as the franchise expanded. Noncitizen voting raises a question unanswered in the modern era: Can voting be detached from citizenship?

Employment and Occupational Privileges

A second area in which the government restricts privileges of noncitizens relative to citizens is in terms of occupational access. These restrictions limit access to certain jobs to citizens and limit some professions requiring a license to citizens. These restrictions appear at both the federal and state levels and apply very differently to permanent residents and the undocumented. Permanent residents have extensive employment privileges in the **private sector**, but they face heavy restrictions on most **public sector** employment.

Restrictions on Employment of the Undocumented. The undocumented face the most severe restrictions. Beginning in 1986 as part of the Immigration Reform and Control Act, it became illegal to employ an undocumented immigrant. With perfect enforcement, then, almost all undocumented immigrants would lose their jobs. The complete enforcement of these "**employer sanctions**" thus absolutely denies employers the right to employ the undocumented. The goal of this legislation was to discourage potential undocumented immigrants from migrating in the first place by removing the incentive of employment.

In practice, enforcement of employer sanctions is erratic. As a result, estimates suggest that approximately 5 million undocumented immigrants resided in the United States in 1996 (U.S. Immigration and Naturalization Service 1997, table P). Although this is the latest reliable estimate of their numbers, it is safe to suggest that this number increases by approximately 300,000 each year.

Public Sector Employment of Permanent Residents.   Permanent resident immigrants face less severe restrictions on occupational access. Those that they do face are relatively more severe in the public sector than in the private sector and restrict permanent residents with specialized professional skills more than average workers.

The public sector enforces many barriers to the employment of permanent residents. The federal government restricts most of its jobs to U.S. citizens. States and localities vary in their employment practices. Most, however, restrict public safety positions, such as police and fire protection, and education positions, including teaching in the public schools, to U.S. citizens.

The origins of these restrictions vary. Some emerged from turn-of-the-century **Progressive Era reforms.** Others, including the restrictions placed on federal employment, appeared during the period of low immigration (but rapid growth in the federal government) between the 1930s and early 1960s. The Progressive reformers sought to restrict the power of the urban machines. One tool for this was to restrict machine leaders' abilities to reward their supporters with municipal employment. This was achieved in part through **civil service requirements** that potential employees demonstrate the skills necessary to hold their jobs and the instituting of employment protections for periods when the government's elected leadership changed, but it was more directly apparent in the creation of absolute barriers to the employment of noncitizens.

Since the decline of the political machines, the justifications for public sector restrictions on noncitizen employment have shifted to concerns about national security and political loyalty. These related concerns increased dramatically during the anticommunist Red Scare of the 1940s and 1950s. All Americans were suspect, especially those with ties to Europe, particularly Southern and Eastern Europe. During this period, federal agencies and many states increasingly expanded barriers to noncitizen employment. With certain exceptions (employment abroad, skilled positions that could not be filled with citizen-workers, national security positions, and the military), all federal agencies have denied permanent residents federal jobs since the 1960s (5 CFR Sec. 338.101).

Restrictions on Professional Licensing.   Governmental restrictions on employment take a second form: restrictions on professional licensing. As most licensing in the United States is under the jurisdiction of state and local governments, this form of occupational control is felt mostly at those levels. These restrictions extend from professions requiring extensive training (e.g., in the legal, medical, and dental fields) to those requiring licenses but much less training (e.g., beautician, barber, or mortician's assistant). These restrictions vary from state to state and tend to be felt more strongly in states with large immigrant populations. Citizens in these professions, through their professional associations, lobby to restrict noncitizen access to the licenses. Often they justify these restrictions by citing concerns that training abroad is not functionally equivalent to that offered in the United States and that professional standards in other countries are lower. These skill and training concerns are reinforced by linguistic arguments. Professional regulators and members of professional associations express concerns that immigrants do not speak English well enough. Either of these sets of concerns could be addressed through testing requirements—to assess knowledge, experience, or language skills—but subtle anti-immigrant messages and the power of the professions in state legislatures often prove sufficient to deny immigrants the opportunity to conduct their professions.

The impact of limiting opportunities to transfer job skills in professions requiring licensing clearly does not influence all immigrants equally. The impact of these sorts of restrictions on international occupational mobility influences those immigrants with more education and more skilled job experience and those who migrate from nations with an extensively developed professional class. Cuban immigrants, for example, faced extensive restrictions on access to the professions in Florida in the 1960s and 1970s. Similar restrictions have been applied to Asian immigrants in California over the past one hundred years.

These public sector efforts to restrict the ability of foreign professionals to carry on their professions once they migrate to the United States should not suggest that the United States seeks to limit the migration of *all* skilled immigrants. Instead, the United States selectively encourages the immigration of certain professionals. As we indicated in Chapter 2, approximately one-third of immigrant visas are allocated to immigrants based on labor skills and not on family unification ideals. This employment-related share of the pool of visas has been steadily growing over the past ten years. Immigration law often specifies the skills being sought. These occupational visas reward those professions with a widespread perception of popular need and those representing more narrow interests. Since World War II, for example, the immigration law has always contained special provisions for the immigration of doctors. In the early 1950s, more narrow interests appeared in the allocation of almost one thousand visas to sheepherders (66 *Statutes at Large* 50, enacted April 9, 1952). Thus, public sector exclusion of permanent resident employment and access of permanent residents to the professions is tempered by the presence of a small pool of immigrants with needed job skills.

Private Sector Employment of Permanent Residents.   The law does not allow the private sector anything near the latitude it does to the public sector to restrict employment opportunities of permanent residents. In fact, most private sector jobs are open to permanent residents.

Federal law offers contradictory protections and limitations in terms of private sector employment. The first principle is the right to equal protection, or nondiscrimination. For the most part, private sector employers cannot discriminate *absolutely* based on citizenship status. In other words, they cannot absolutely exclude permanent residents from employment. Congress modified this principle of nondiscrimination in 1986 with a form of sanctioned discrimination. Beginning that year, private sector employers who have equally qualified job candidates, one of whom is a citizen and one of whom is a permanent resident, may select the citizen without fear of losing a discrimination suit (100 *Statutes at Large* 3359, enacted November 6, 1986). Although this may seem to be a minor restriction on the job opportunities of permanent residents, it deserves more than a passing mention: It is one of very few U.S. laws that explicitly sanctions discrimination against a named population.

In addition to this sanctioning of discrimination against permanent residents, Congress has recognized a special category of private sector jobs that can exclude noncitizens. This category includes employment with contractors doing work for the government in areas related to national security. Overall, this includes several million jobs, including those engaged in by Defense Department contractors. The justification for the exclusion of noncitizens from these jobs is similar to the rationale used to exclude them from government employment. Their loyalty is in doubt and, as a result, they cannot be offered these jobs.

In sum, employment and professional opportunities for immigrants vary considerably, based both on immigrant status and on what type of employment the immigrant seeks. The nation bars the undocumented from all employment, though it fails to enforce the prohibition rigorously. Permanent residents, by contrast, face few formal restrictions on private sector employment, though they can face legal discrimination when competing against a U.S. citizen. Many permanent residents with professional skills that require licensing, however, are denied the opportunity to earn these licenses based on their citizenship status. As a result, they cannot practice their profession. Finally, permanent residents are barred from many public sector jobs. Thus, employment and occupational rights and privileges compose a second area in which the privileges of immigrants are different from those of the U.S.-born.

Programmatic Privileges in Federal Government Programs

The most hotly debated area of public policy in which citizen and noncitizen privileges differ is that of access to federal government social welfare programs. We call such access "programmatic privileges," meaning the ability to participate in federal and state programs designed to meet the needs of the population. The programs most debated are social welfare programs such as food stamps, Temporary Aid to Needy Families (formerly Aid to Families with Dependent Children, under which cash and services are provided to low-income households with children under age eighteen), Medicaid (health insurance for low-income households), and Supplemental Security Income (a cash assistance program for low-income elderly persons). These four programs are mandated by the federal government and paid for by federal and state taxes to provide a safety net for the economically disadvantaged.

The debate over immigrant access to programmatic privileges is distinct from the other two areas that we have discussed thus far in this chapter. Both voting and employment/professional rights and privileges have long been a part of the national discussion on immigrant settlement. As we have already mentioned, many states granted voting rights to immigrants around the turn of the century. Similarly, in that same era, municipal governments employed some immigrants. Since the federal government was small during this era, municipal employment was the major form of public sector employment. Progressive organization against the urban machines began the process of immigrant employment restriction that we see today. The national debate over immigrant programmatic privileges, however, could not begin until after these programs were created, first under the **New Deal** in the 1930s and particularly through the **Great Society** projects of the 1960s.

The creation and expansion of federal and state guarantees to food and to such services as health care and housing came during a period of relatively low immigration. During the initial establishment of the social safety net in the 1930s, few immigrated to the United States and some previous immigrants were deported. These deportations of Mexicans were justified in part as a response to the cost of providing relief. When the federal government created the first national social insurance programs in the 1930s such as Social Security, the needs of immigrants were not part of the debate. Similarly in the 1960s, with Great Society programs such as the expansion of AFDC and the creation of Medicaid, immigration was low and the cost of providing immigrant eligibility for these programs was also low.

The steady increase in the cost of the social safety net, however, has spurred a steady restriction on immigrant access to federal programs. These limitations on immigrant access are particularly felt in programs that are **needs-tested** (in which eligibility is determined by need, that is, by income below a designated threshold), such as AFDC or Medicaid. Restrictions on immigrant rights and privileges in **contributory programs** are fewer. Contributory programs are those such as Medicare or Social Security, in which the benefit is related to contributions made to the program, though the contribution may not pay for the benefit.

Advocates of denying permanent residents eligibility to federal social welfare programs have made three arguments. The first is cost. Congress is seeking to cut the cost of **entitlement programs**. These are programs in which spending is determined by the total demand generated by people meeting the income threshold. Thus, to cut the cost of the program, Congress must change the eligibility criteria. If costs have to be cut, some argue that the government has a greater responsibility to citizens. Thus, the pain of cuts can be reduced to citizens by denying benefits to noncitizens. From a political perspective, this strategy of budget cutting has a second advantage to Congress. Noncitizens are not voters, so electoral backlash is less likely if noncitizen benefits are cut. This budgetary impact is great. One-half of the $55 billion in savings in the 1996 Welfare Reform Bill was achieved simply by making cuts in services to noncitizens.

A second, more theoretical, observation offers a principled justification for denying benefits to permanent residents. Supporters of benefit restrictions observe that access to social welfare programs may slow the process of immigrant adaptation and acculturation. Offered as examples are some recent groups of refugees, such as the Hmong and Cambodians from Southeast Asia. Congress granted these refugees social safety net program eligibility as well as special refugee assistance programs. Despite these various forms of assistance, these groups remained in poverty and have become disproportionately dependent on public aid. Thus, some critics of government social welfare spending on immigrants argue that denying benefits is actually beneficial to their long-term advance. This position, though frequently argued by the political right, also taps immigrant-advocate rhetoric about no immigrant coming to the United States for benefits. If, as these immigrant advocates argue, no immigrant comes to the United States to receive assistance and, in fact, simply wants the opportunity to succeed, then the denial of benefits is not a problem.

The third argument made in support of denying immigrants federal benefits transfers the responsibility for caring for the immigrant from the federal government to the person who petitioned for the admission of the immigrant. The sponsor promises to support the immigrant during the immigrant's period of transition to citizenship. Prior to the 1996 reforms, the sponsor's income was added to the immigrant's to determine whether the immigrant was eligible for AFDC, SSI, and food stamps for the first three to five years after immigration. However, as we have suggested, the sponsor's promise was not legally binding. Under the 1996 amendments to the Immigration and Welfare Reform Bills, the sponsor's responsibility was extended to covering the first ten years of permanent residence and to making a legally binding commitment.

Opponents of limitations to permanent resident eligibility for social welfare benefits have not developed a comprehensive response to these three claims. Instead, they base their support on humanitarian grounds and on the empirical observation that few immigrants use these programs. The humanitarian argument is straightforward. Congress designed these programs to address the needs of the poor in the society. If the poverty is sufficiently severe, then, permanent residents should be eligible. The argument for this eligibility is particularly strong when the cause of the poverty is something that happened after immigration, such as illness or disability. Empirically, opponents of benefits cuts note that the current law bars many recent immigrants from program eligibility. Therefore, no immigrant will migrate with the intention of earning benefits. Thus, if the society wants to continue to ameliorate the effect of poverty in the society, it must respond to the needs of long-term permanent residents. With the exception of emergency medical services, few extend this argument to addressing the social welfare needs of the undocumented.

Studies indicate that the more generous system of social welfare program eligibility available before 1996 did not spur social welfare dependence among permanent residents. Several studies have demonstrated that social welfare utilization rates are lower for permanent residents than for the population as a whole. There was one exception: Elderly immigrants had high utilization rates for SSI, Medicaid, and Medicare. Although elderly immigrants lost access to SSI in 1996, Congress restored their benefits in 1997.

Although this has not been discussed in the congressional debates, there is a final argument against linking social welfare benefits to citizenship. Such a linkage would create an instrumental motivation to naturalize. In other words, if the only way that immigrants could assure that they would be protected in times of poverty would be to naturalize, then they would be much more likely to become citizens as soon as they become eligible. This goal may be laudable, but the reasons may strike some as less than laudable. As we showed in Chapter 3, naturalization has sought to measure political attachment to the United States through a knowledge-based test. Although the formal standards are minimal, the citizen population has largely welcomed the voluntary citizens. However, if citizens were to come to perceive immigrants seeking naturalization as simply doing so to become eligible for federal benefits, the support for the nation's voluntary citizens could dissolve.

These arguments about the advisability of continuing to provide social welfare benefits to permanent residents played little role in the outcome of the legislative debate. Instead, budget concerns drove congressional decisionmaking.

In the Personal Responsibility and Work Opportunity Reconciliation Act of 1996 (110 *Statutes at Large* 2105, enacted August 22, 1996), Congress eliminated immigrant eligibility for food stamps and SSI. They left to the states the responsibility for determining immigrant eligibility for Medicaid and TANF. States granting immigrants benefits under these programs, however, had to pay the costs from their own budgets or from savings in citizen use of these programs (see Table 4.1).

In what must have proved a surprise for advocates of cutting immigrants from eligibility for social welfare benefits, there was a political price paid for these cuts. In the 1996 elections, Latinos and Asian Americans voted for the Democrats at higher than average rates. One of the explanations for these voting patterns was the perception in these ethnic communities that immigrants were being made into scapegoats and that these policy changes would slow the process of immigrant incorporation. President Clinton, despite having signed the Welfare Reform Bill, captured this sentiment by promising, at the signing, to work to restore some benefits to permanent residents. In 1997, with little organized opposition, Congress restored SSI benefits to elderly immigrants.

Conclusions on Immigrant Rights, Privileges, and Responsibilities

U.S. society has created a separate statutory niche for immigrants and then, among immigrants, has distinguished between permanent residents and the undocumented. Permanent residents are entitled to many but not all of the rights and privileges of U.S. citizens. They are denied equal employment, particularly in the public sector, and many programmatic benefits. The chasm between the undocumented and the U.S. citizen population is much greater. Although the undocumented are entitled to basic civil and procedural rights under the Constitution, they are denied most statutory privileges and face the continual threat of deportation. Formally, they may not work in the United States, though many do. Most federal social welfare programs also bar their participation. Both permanent residents and undocumented immigrants are almost completely excluded from the franchise.

TABLE 4.1 Changes in Immigrant Eligibility for Federal Social Welfare Programs with the Passage of the Personal Responsibility and Work Opportunity Reconciliation Act of 1996 (1996 Welfare Reform Bill)

	1996 and Before			After 1996		
	Program Eligibility For			Program Eligibility For		
Program	Permanent Residents	Refugees	Undocumented Immigrants	Permanent Residents	Refugees	Undocumented Immigrants
Cash Assistance						
AFDC/TANF[a]	Yes, after 3 years[b]	Yes	No	No, during first 5 years; after up to states	Yes, first 5 years; after, up to states	No
SSI	Yes, after 5 years[b]	Yes	No	No/Yes, after 5 years[d]	Yes, first 5 years; after No/Yes[d]	No
Unemployment insurance	Yes	Yes	No	Yes	Yes	No
Medical Care						
Medicaid	Yes	Yes	Only emergency services	State option and emergency services	Yes, first 5 years; after, state option and emergency services	Only emergency services
Food						
Food stamps	Yes, after 3 years[b]	Yes	No[c]	No	Yes, first 5 years; after No	No
School lunch and breakfast	Yes	Yes	Yes	Yes	Yes	Yes

Education						
Head Start	Yes	Yes	Yes	Yes	Yes	Yes
College loans	Yes	Yes	No	Yes	Yes	No
JTPA	Yes	Yes	Yes	Yes	Yes	Yes

Key:

AFDC   Aid to Families with Dependent Children
JTPA   Job Training and Partnership Act
SSI   Supplemental Security Income
TANF   Temporary Aid to Needy Families

[a]Aid to Families with Dependent Children (AFDC) changed to Temporary Aid to Needy Families in the Personal Responsibility and Work Opportunity Reconciliation Act of 1996.

[b]Eligibility can be established earlier if sponsor is eligible for programmatic benefits.

[c]Eligibility established by citizenship or residency status of the child.

[d]Cuts to SSI restored in 1997.

Source: National Immigration Law Center, 1994, xi; 1996, 1 (1).

This exclusion from full integration into the civil society based on citizenship status has evolved for different reasons in each of the policy areas. Exclusion from voting rights has been justified through a definition of membership in the polity, a connection between citizenship and having a stake in the society that merits a voice in its future. Exclusion from employment rights and privileges, however, developed in response to fears of immigrants. These fears included their potential corrupting influence and their potential disloyalty. Finally, financial considerations in times of increasing concern about the costs of social welfare programs justified the exclusion from programmatic benefits. The desire for cost savings did include a principled foundation to these considerations: the desire not to impede immigrants' acculturation. In making reductions in immigrant program eligibility, however, the evidence of the impact of the availability of benefits on immigrant adaptation was rarely debated.

U.S. society, then, has developed three barriers to keep immigrants in a secondary status—membership, loyalty, and cost. After five years, permanent resident immigrants may overcome these barriers through naturalization, an act that proves their membership, their loyalty, and their value to the society. The barriers for undocumented immigrants are greater and cannot be overcome through a pledge of membership.

The States and the Settlement Process

Throughout our discussion of immigrants' rights, privileges, and responsibilities, we have focused on the federal government. In the late twentieth century, it has primary policymaking responsibility for immigrant incorporation by setting the standards for immigration and naturalization and by determining social welfare program eligibility. Increasingly, however, the states are seeking anew to become involved in the process.

We assess three dimensions of this effort at restructuring the federalist relationship. First, we examine the most common state claim, which is primarily fiscal. Several states have filed suit to recoup the expenses of providing state services to undocumented immigrants. However, one state has sought to involve itself more directly in policymaking. This is the second dimension of state government involvement in settlement examined in this section. California's voters in 1994 supported Proposition 187 by a margin of two to one. Aside from specific limitations on services to immigrants, this proposition can be viewed as an effort to transfer power over immigration enforcement to state officials. Finally, we examine one component of Proposition 187 that suggests some of the long-term costs in expanding the debate over immigrants to the states. States may try to cut the most costly service provided to immigrants: primary and secondary education.

Who Pays for Undocumented Immigrants?

Over the past few years, several states have filed suit against the federal government to recoup the costs of providing services to undocumented immigrants. These states—including California, Florida, and Texas—argue that since the federal government is responsible for the protection of the borders, it should be responsible for the costs of its failures. To date, all such efforts have been rebuffed by the federal courts.

The suits have sought reimbursement for a variety of costs. The largest among these was the cost of providing education to undocumented children and the states' shares of federal social welfare programs such as Medicaid and food stamps. Some states have also sought reimbursement for emergency medical services in public hospitals and the costs of incarceration of undocumented immigrants. Each state's suit sought more than $1 billion in reimbursements for several years' worth of services.

The goals of the states have been varied and must, in part, be seen as fiscal opportunism. When the attorney general of Texas filed suit, for example, he noted that he was taking no position on undocumented immigration. Instead, he reported that he would be derelict if he failed to pursue such a lucrative opportunity for Texas while other states might benefit if they were to win suits against the federal government and Texas did not, only because it had not filed suit.

Failure in the courts has not meant that these efforts have been without impact. Congress has appropriated funds to offset partially the states' costs in providing services to the undocumented. These funds account for a small percentage of the billions sought by the states. Yet, their appropriation in times of slow growth in federal spending reflects the fact that Congress recognized the legitimacy of state demands or, at least, the resonance of these claims with voters.

The long-term impact is perhaps greater than the small amount of money that has been appropriated. As we will indicate in a subsequent discussion, Congress considered (and rejected) an unprecedented *de*centralization of federal control over settlement policy. Specifically, it reviewed legislation that would have allowed states to deny education to the children of undocumented immigrants. This legislation passed the House of Representatives, but failed in the Senate.

As our discussion so far in this chapter indicates, Congress has consistently held states to higher standards than the federal government in terms of limiting rights and privileges of noncitizens. This proposal concerning education would have reversed this long-standing pattern, allowing the states to decide in this one key area what level of service they want to provide. Were similar legislation to be considered by Congress and pass, congressional initiatives to allow states to determine immigrant programmatic eligibility could become more common and be extended to permanent residents as well as the undocumented. Such decentralization could fundamentally change the pattern of U.S. immigrant settlement.

Proposition 187

The impetus for the first of the state suits to recoup the cost of providing services to the undocumented was popular concern in California about the numbers and costs of undocumented immigration. This concern drove the suit against the federal government, but it also took the form of an activity in which the mass electorate could participate—a state initiative numbered 187, or Proposition 187, as it came to be known in the press.

Before getting into the specifics of the proposition, we should note that the California political environment is unique for several reasons. These unique characteristics united to force the immigration issue onto the national agenda in a way that had not occurred since the passage of the National Origin Quota Acts in the 1920s. As we will suggest, it allowed immigration and settlement policy to reflect mass interests, as opposed to reflecting the elite and employer interests that usually shape policies in this area.

The first factor is California's sheer size and commensurate importance in presidential politics. More than one in ten Americans (nearly 30 million out of the nation's 250 million people in 1990) live in the state. With fifty-four **Electoral College** votes, it offers one-fifth of the needed number to become president. Thus, its interests get an immediate hearing in Washington.

A second unique characteristic is California's long-term love-hate relationship with immigrants, particularly those from Mexico. Throughout much of its history, California has actively encouraged immigration. In the twentieth century, California's political and economic leaders battled efforts to increase enforcement of immigration law. Today, it has the largest number of foreign-born residents of any state. Approximately 6.5 million out of the 19.8 million foreign-born individuals counted in the 1990 census resided in California (U.S. Bureau of the Census 1993b, table 1). Its leaders, including Governor Pete Wilson, who spearheaded the effort to pass Proposition 187, have actively lobbied in Washington to assure that California agricultural interests have had access to a continuous supply of cheap immigrant labor. Despite this continuing demand, California has periodically turned against the immigrant, leading to widespread deportation of Mexicans in the 1930s and agricultural labor in the 1950s. This love-hate relationship reflects, in part, a divergence that exists nationally between elite and employer attitudes toward immigration, which are generally supportive, and mass attitudes, which are often much more ambivalent and frequently hostile.

The final unique feature of California that made it the epicenter of the current national concern about immigration is the **initiative** process. In California, individuals may organize to place propositions on the state ballot. If they are successful in getting the issue on the ballot and passed by the electorate, the resulting laws have a standing above statutes passed by the legislature and can only be reversed by constitutional amendment or another initiative that explicitly reverses the first. To many, the initiative process has elements of direct democracy that compensate for the weaknesses of Madisonian representative democracy. The initiative process, however, is not without its problems. Organized interests are able to use the process to circumvent elected leaders and then buy support for controversial positions. Of equal concern, many propositions do not receive much popular attention, so the electorate is ill-informed. Finally, initiatives are sometimes placed on the ballot strategically to lure specific electorates to vote for or against a separate initiative or a candidate.

These unique features of California politics came together in November 1994, when California voters passed Proposition 187 by a margin of approximately two to one. Despite being an off-year election, turnout was high. Preelection polling demonstrated that voters were aware of Proposition 187 and that relatively few were neutral on it. Both advocates and opponents used extensive television advertising to make their case. The advocates had both a financial advantage and two statewide campaigns that reinforced the message of controlling the borders. Both Governor Pete Wilson and senatorial candidate Michael Huffington used advertisements with an immigrant-control theme. It is not an overstatement to say that each hour during the month before the campaign, a television viewer or radio listener would see or hear several messages that either explicitly endorsed Proposition 187 or spoke of the need to control borders.

Opponents of the proposition were slower to organize. Although opponents included many California civic leaders, neither of the Democratic statewide candidates—Kathleen Brown and Dianne Feinstein—used her campaign to mobilize against the initiative. The one resource that opponents had was mobilized ethnic populations. Although California's Latino and Asian populations did vote at record numbers, they were not able to overcome equally high mobilization among non-Hispanic whites who supported the proposition (Tomás Rivera Center 1996).

The proposition makes three claims:

The People of California find and declare as follows:
That they have suffered and are suffering economic hardship caused by the presence of illegal aliens in this state. That they have suffered and are suffering personal injury and damage caused by the criminal conduct of illegal aliens in this state. That they have the right to the protection of their government from any person or persons entering this country unlawfully. (Preamble to California Proposition 187)

In order to address these concerns, the proposition called for the exclusion of undocumented immigrants from public social services and health care services, the exclusion of undocumented immigrant children from public elementary and secondary schools and public colleges and universities, the criminalization of the manufacture or use of false citizenship or resident alien documents, and the promise of added cooperation between state agencies and the INS. This final cooperation provision would require local governments to turn suspected undocumented immigrants over to federal authorities.

Within a day of the proposition's passage, opponents sought and received a federal court injunction to halt its implementation. This ruling was appealed and upheld. With the exception of the provisions concerning the manufacture and use of false residency or citizenship documents, no aspect of the proposition has been implemented, and few believe that its major provisions will be held constitutional.

Nevertheless, its importance should not be underrated. Politically, it raised mass concerns about immigration in a manner that had not been seen since the reform of the immigration law in 1965. Equally important, it brought immigration into the national political debates in 1996. The unique features of California's political system and attitudes toward immigration may in part explain why this issue erupted when and where it did, but California citizens' attitudes toward immigration, and particularly undocumented immigration, are not that different from those held by citizens of other states. In fact, citizens' groups in several other states (most notably Florida, Texas, and Arizona) tried but failed to enact measures similar to Proposition 187. Had these states had initiative procedures similar to California, these efforts would likely have succeeded.

Aside from political considerations, the legacy of Proposition 187 is important for a second reason. It offers a strategy for immigration control that might well come to be adopted if national leaders seek more rigorous enforcement of immigration law. Proposition 187 made *all* state and local government employees, including teachers and medical personnel, immigration enforcement agents. It required that these officials check identity papers prior to teaching or providing a service. Were this expanded monitoring and enforcement to become national policy, it would fundamentally shift the locus for settlement policy from the federal government to the states and localities.

As should be evident from our discussions in Chapters 2 and 3, this would amount to a return to the pattern of the nineteenth century, with one major change. In the nineteenth century, local governments wanted immigrants, though those that received large numbers worried that penniless immigrants would become a social burden. Their labor was valuable to economic development, and with few public services, their cost was nil. Today, with the expansion in services, this equation is changed. Some states and localities would still seek immigrants, but others, fearing their cost, would use their enforcement powers to keep immigrants away. The impetus to nationalize the delivery of naturalization and settlement assistance could be lost to local fiscal concerns.

Public Education and Undocumented Immigrants

Our discussion of programmatic benefits and immigrant rights and privileges has primarily focused on federal programs and permanent residents. As we have suggested, the undocumented are barred from almost all federal social welfare benefits. This prohibition extends to contributory programs, such as unemployment compensation (90 *Statutes at Large* 2706, enacted October 20, 1976). In the current political environment, there appears to be little interest in changing this pattern. The cost, however, of an undocumented immigrant population is felt more at the state and local levels and, particularly, in the provision of primary and secondary education.

The Supreme Court has ruled that it is unconstitutional for the states to deny education to the undocumented, though the Court held out the possibility that the federal government could establish such a bar. In *Plyler v. Doe* (457 U.S. 202 [1982]), the Supreme Court held that undocumented immigrant children have a constitutional right to education, as long as it is being offered to others and as long as Congress has not asserted responsibility in this area. The nature of the Supreme Court majority in this decision—a series of loosely related concurring opinions, the convoluted argument made in support of this right, and the failure of Texas (the state being sued in the case) to assert that there was a compelling state interest in denying education to undocumented immigrant children—has led many observers to think that the Supreme Court would be open to a renewed effort to deny education to undocumented children. This effort appears in California's Proposition 187. It also appears in legislation introduced by Representative Elton Gallegly (R–CA) in 1995 to allow states to limit educational services based on citizenship status. This bill passed the House of Representatives and was endorsed by 1996 Republican presidential nominee Bob Dole. Although it failed to pass the Senate, similar legislation will likely be proposed during less flush economic periods.

Whether these efforts are symbolic or practical, they raise a question that does not appear so clearly in the other discussions of differential access to programmatic benefits based on citizenship status. Denying education to undocumented children has a long-term consequence—and not just for the state denying benefits—that the society will have to pay for. Whereas other government services can be compensated for—by family, by the immigrant's sponsor, by the immigrant community, by community philanthropic organizations, or by charity—public education for a large pool of undocumented immigrants cannot be replaced by nongovernment sources. To the extent that advocates justify this change on a budgetary basis, the long-term costs must be calculated as well. Arguably, states are not in as strong a position to judge these costs as is the federal government.

Conclusions on Settlement Policy and Federalism

The steady expansion of immigration beginning in the 1960s continues in the 1990s. But the debate around immigration has shifted in this decade. The large number of immigrants—both documented and undocumented—raises questions about what rights, privileges, and responsibilities the society chooses to offer. The federal government denies certain, but limited, electoral, employment, and programmatic rights and privileges to noncitizens. For the most part, it has restricted state and private sector efforts to do the same. It is at the state and local levels, however, that the day-to-day process of settlement occurs. As these governments have been asked to share a greater burden of settlement, they have begun to ask for greater responsibility in deciding what rights and responsibilities immigrants in their states should have. To date, this call for a shift in the balance between the federal government and state governments has focused primarily on the undocumented immigrant and, perhaps, will not extend to permanent residents. Regardless of exactly who is the focus, these new efforts by states to enter the debate over settlement potentially represent a major change in the direction of immigration, naturalization, and settlement efforts in the United States.

Immigrants and Minorities

Immigration to the United States does not occur in a vacuum. From their first days in the United States, immigrants interact with other immigrants and with U.S.-born populations and reshape what it means to be American for all involved. For reasons that we will explore, the impact of immigrants is particularly strong in one segment of U.S. society—the U.S.-born minority population (what we will call minorities). In using the term "minorities," we mean racial and ethnic minorities and, particularly, African Americans.

This interaction between immigrants and minorities has some tangible foundations. Equally important, the interaction between immigrants and minorities offers insights into the way the society tries to address public policy needs disproportionately experienced by disadvantaged groups within the society. As we have indicated, the needs of U.S.-born minorities and immigrants are different, though the public policies developed for immigrant populations often follow those developed for minorities.

The tangible foundations of immigrant and minority interaction in U.S. society involve geography, ethnicity, and class. Overwhelmingly, immigration since 1965 has been an urban phenomenon. Within cities, immigrants often live in specific neighborhoods. Thus, geographically, most immigrant populations come into immediate contact with minority populations often before they have sustained contact with nonminority natives. These U.S.-born populations are often dominated by coethnics. An immigrant from Mexico will therefore likely live around and work with both U.S.-born citizens of Mexican ancestry and other Mexican immigrants. Finally, class dictates that immigrants and minorities interact. The majority of immigrants are at the lower end of the economic spectrum. Again, this puts them into contact with U.S.-born minorities, particularly in the urban environment. This contact is not just interpersonal. Immigrants' class position dictates that they are in a position to benefit from policies designed to assist U.S.-born populations in poverty. As there is little explicit assistance from the society with settlement, these public policies become a de facto settlement policy.

This connection between immigrants and U.S.-born minorities raises a dilemma for the polity. It becomes easy to view these populations as being one because they have common needs. Thus, society applies the same set of public policy solutions to both populations. Instead, however, the differences between the two populations are great, and the needs of immigrants may well be different from those of minorities. Society, however, has not recognized this difference. Instead, it has dealt with this issue by extending to immigrants programs that were designed to assist minorities and to remedy past discrimination against minorities. Undeniably, immigrants have benefited from these programs in the short term, while the cost to minorities has not been great. Nevertheless, it does both populations a disservice: Programs for minorities are diluted, and immigrant needs are not met with carefully crafted public policies.

Public Policy Slippage Between Immigrants and Minorities

During the same period that many social welfare programs emerged, the United States also developed group-based programs targeted at groups that had experienced discrimination in the past. Initially designed to remedy past discrimination against African Americans, these programs—civil rights and voting rights protections and affirmative action programs—were soon expanded to ethnic populations that had also experienced discrimination in the past. These included Latinos, Asian Americans, and Native Americans. These remedial programs are the exception in American political history, where policy had explicitly or, more often, implicitly benefited society's dominant population. These remedial programs have been highly controversial and, at this writing, are being attacked in the courts and in legislatures.

What has been less noticed is that immigrants have come to benefit from these programs since their inception. An example appears in the **Voting Rights Act of 1965**, which we alluded to earlier. In its initial form, the act sought to remove barriers to registration and voting experienced by African Americans. Ten years later, Congress extended these same provisions to other U.S. populations that had experienced discrimination: Latinos (based largely on discrimination against Mexican Americans and Puerto Ricans), Asians (based on discrimination against Chinese Americans, Japanese Americans, and Filipino Americans), Native Americans, and Alaskan Natives. Congress mandated new electoral resources unique to the form of discrimination they experienced and provided them with bilingual registration and election materials.

Congress further amended the legislation in 1982 to add to the VRA's mandate. After 1982, minority communities not only had protections against electoral exclusion but also received a guarantee that their votes could not be diluted by districting strategies. The practical consequence of this guarantee was that in areas where minority populations are concentrated, officeholder districts must be drawn with majority-minority populations to increase the likelihood of a minority officeholder. The courts are now questioning the constitutionality of this guarantee, but all districts drawn after the 1990 census were influenced by these requirements.

Since the passage of the VRA, the African-American population has expanded only slightly through immigration. Latino and Asian populations, however, have seen considerable immigration. Thus, there are many people who receive the protection of the VRA who could not have been discriminated against before the passage of the act because they did not yet live in the United States.

The same pattern of immigrant beneficiaries appears in affirmative action programs designed to improve minority access to employment, education, and government contracting. Some of today's beneficiaries include immigrants who could not have experienced the discrimination Congress designed these programs to remedy.

Immigrant access to programs designed to remedy past discrimination against minorities raises questions for the polity, among them questions of equity, effectiveness, and backlash. In terms of equity, minority communities could well resent the dilution of these programs. In an era of limited resources, affirmative action programs may reward well-trained immigrants over U.S.-born coethnics or African Americans who have experienced discrimination in the United States and who were the intended beneficiaries of the program. Equity issues may also be raised for nonminority populations that may (or may not) grudgingly accept the Voting Rights Act and affirmative action programs but will be opposed to the extension of these remedial programs to immigrants.

A second question that must be asked about the extension of programs designed for minorities to immigrants concerns effectiveness. We have indicated that the nation offers little in terms of a formal settlement policy for immigrants; instead, it offers opportunities to individual immigrants through naturalization. Remedial programs, however, have come to be seen by some immigrant leaders as a substitute for a well-developed settlement policy. In the absence of a settlement policy, these programs may be a useful substitute. Congress did not, however, design them with the intent of addressing immigrant needs. If immigrant leaders or policymakers advocate a set of policies specifically designed to speed or ease the transition of immigrants into equal citizens, they should design and implement such a policy and not simply rely on expedient borrowing from minority programs.

The final concern—backlash—is implicit in the first two issues. Opponents of remedial programs have used the expansion of the program's beneficiaries as a tool to undermine popular and policymaker support. Evidence of this appears in the Voting Rights Act. As we have indicated, Congress mandated bilingual election materials as a tool to remedy discrimination (particularly educational discrimination) against Latinos and Asians. Today, however, many interpret these ballots as a tool of immigrant empowerment. If these concerns are used to undermine the VRA, then concerns about immigrants will take away a hard-won program that benefits minorities. Similar concerns are being raised about immigrant beneficiaries of affirmative action programs.

Conclusions on Public Policy Slippage

The slippage of public policies designed for minority populations to immigrant communities has a more insidious side. It puts these two populations in competition both for public resources and for public sympathy. The needs of minority populations have become partially lost in the growing debate over immigration. As vitriolic as some of the rhetoric has been about immigrants, the society continues to regard them favorably as compared to minorities, particularly African Americans. Thus, reasoned debate about the public policy needs of each population has been lost. The absence, then, of a U.S. settlement policy may soon be matched by the absence of a U.S. policy to assist U.S.-born minority populations.

Mediating the Needs of Immigrants and Natives

This discussion of the relationship between immigrants and natives suggests the complexity of the dilemma identified in this chapter, that is, the tension between immigrants' public policy needs and those of the U.S.-born. First, as a nation of immigrants, U.S. society must continually reassess what rights, privileges, and responsibilities it chooses to extend to immigrants and what immigrants have to do to earn these rights and privileges. Relatedly, it must decide what immigrants must sacrifice in terms of their culture and identity to achieve rights and privileges in U.S. society. Second, U.S. society must evaluate whether to treat immigrants as individuals or members of a group (or groups). Thus, once society has decided what rights and responsibilities to extend to immigrants, it must assess whether these go to individuals or to groups. Finally, the society must decide whether it needs a comprehensive settlement policy or, instead, to determine with each piece of legislation whether immigrants should be treated like others in U.S. society.

Mode of Immigrant Incorporation

At present, U.S. society has developed a three-tiered system for immigrant civic participation: Different rights and privileges accrue to naturalized citizens, legal permanent residents, and undocumented immigrants. At one extreme, full membership is offered. At the other, most rights, privileges, and government services (with the exception of education) are denied. After five years, permanent residents become eligible for full membership. Unless they can regularize their status, undocumented immigrants are consigned permanently to the excluded category (though erratic enforcement assures that this exclusion is not complete). In between are non-naturalized permanent residents who have access to many of the rights, privileges, and responsibilities of citizens but have explicitly been excluded from most electoral rights and some employment and programmatic privileges.

What is asked in return from the immigrant? From the naturalized citizens, the society asks for political loyalty and civic knowledge. The naturalization exam tests knowledge of the United States, its history, and its governmental system. The oath of naturalization requires the immigrant to swear (or affirm) loyalty to the United States and to renounce loyalty to the former sovereign. Although the debate over immigration is often phrased in cultural terms, it is important to notice what this full membership does not *require*, namely, cultural loyalty. The nation requires most naturalizing citizens to know English, but this knowledge is not expected to replace the native language. Thus, to join the United States and to attain full rights in the society is to share in a *political* ideal. Cultural change undoubtedly occurs when immigrants come into contact with natives, but formal political membership and full rights are not determined by these cultural characteristics.

Permanent residents attain many rights and privileges at immigration. These rights and privileges are awarded by meeting the standards of U.S. immigration law. This immigration law does include political considerations (immigrants may not be anarchists or former officials of the Communist or Nazi parties) and some cultural characteristics (the law is now more likely to award some visas to English speakers). For the most part, however, these considerations are minor relative to the complexities of U.S. immigration policy, which focuses more on family and employment than on politics and culture. Thus, the rights and privileges extended to permanent residents emerge from their residential status in the United States. In this case, rights and privileges are tied to residence.

The denial of rights and privileges to undocumented immigrants is the converse of the rights and privileges granted to permanent residents. It should be noted that the undocumented are accorded fundamental constitutional guarantees, including due process guarantees (although local officials often violate these guarantees). For the undocumented, therefore, residence does not guarantee rights or privileges.

Individual Rights Versus Group-Based Rights

A second tension in the settlement of immigrants emerges from the group-based nature of immigration. It is easy to view immigrants as members of a group. We do that in this volume by examining the characteristics of immigration in the aggregate. We speak of national-origin groups making up a period's immigration, we speak of waves of immigration, and we speak of immigrant-ethnic populations in cities or regions. Equally important, the society awards basic rights to groups. The undocumented earn basic constitutional guarantees based upon their presence in the United States. This is a group composed of people physically present in the United States. Permanent residents earn statutory privileges again based on group membership, the group of people admitted to permanent residence. Full membership, however, is individual (or familial for minor children). The individual must petition the government for membership and demonstrate individual qualifications to be a member.

The individual nature of gaining full rights and privileges in the society suggests a necessary direction for a U.S. settlement policy, if the nation chooses to adopt one. Individuals, and not groups, must be empowered to develop political attachments to the United States and to be able to meet the bureaucratic requirements of naturalization. At a minimum, this requires added resources for education, particularly civic education and English-language training. In addition, it indicates the need for assistance with the bureaucratic requirements. As we found in Chapter 3, these educational services are in short supply, and assistance with bureaucratic requirements is largely provided by overtaxed community groups, not by the government. Finally, the U.S. government could reshape its role by promoting the value of U.S. citizenship. As we have mentioned, many permanent residents do not see the benefits of citizenship. To the degree that full membership requires individual and not group action, the government must target its resources in order to empower individuals to assert their membership.

Clearly, the U.S. government faces another option, and that is group-based incorporation. Other immigrant-receiving societies use such policies in part to incorporate immigrants. Australia, for example, sponsors organizations to maintain the cultures of immigrant-ethnic populations such as Italian Australians. These government-sponsored ethnic organizations are given the responsibility to distribute some government resources to fellow ethnics. Such governmental "multicultural" policies maintain ethnic group membership and the cultural connection of the group membership as a way to allocate government resources to encourage membership. Although this is an option for the United States, it would represent a complete reversal of the direction that settlement policy has taken in the past in the United States.

Constructing the Immigrant Experience

The largely private nature of assistance to immigrants designed to assist in achieving formal membership should not obscure the fact that the United States has a de facto settlement policy. Immigrants have come to be the beneficiaries of targeted programs designed to remedy past discrimination against minorities. This de facto policy presents several dilemmas, for immigrants, for U.S.-born minorities, and for the society as a whole.

Although immigrants may benefit in the short term from affirmative action programs and other targeted programs, these programs, as we have demonstrated, do not provide specifically for immigrant needs. Instead, they ameliorate some of the class characteristics of immigrants but they do not necessary assure that immigrants move toward citizenship and full political rights. What has been granted, though, can be taken away, particularly for noncitizens. Clearly, policies such as these might be part of a thoughtful settlement policy, but they do not replace the core need of immigrants to attain full civic rights.

The inclusion of immigrants as beneficiaries in these programs designed for minorities presents a problem for minority leaders. In a time of limited societal resources, immigrants diminish what can be available to remedy past discrimination against minorities. Further, the perception in the dominant society that these programs generate undeserving beneficiaries might lead to the destruction of these efforts. To the extent that these programs genuinely benefit minority populations, this threat of loss presents a dilemma.

Finally, the society faces a potential problem. By not distinguishing immigrants from minorities, the United States runs the risk of encouraging immigrants to behave as minorities, in opposition to the dominant society and making group-based demands of the dominant society. As we suggested in Chapter 2, this "minoritization" has not characterized previous waves of immigrants. Were societal confusion about immigrants to shift the thinking of immigrants, the society as a whole would face a long-term cost. Efforts to deny education to the children of the undocumented (regardless of the child's citizenship status) offer disturbing evidence of this minoritization. It was the denial of education that characterized the discrimination against African Americans, Mexican Americans, Chinese Americans, and Puerto Ricans and that spurred the remedial programs of the 1960s and beyond. If immigrants came to perceive that their denial of access to opportunities in the society was based on their membership in the immigrant group, they could well decide to organize around this identity to demand specific rights and privileges for the group.

Conclusion

Earlier in this volume, we introduced the basic contradiction between popular reverence for immigrants and opposition to immigration. The process of settlement shapes which of these aspects the mass of the citizenry pays attention to when it considers the process of bringing new people into the United States. When settlement is successful, reverence appears. When it is unsuccessful, the citizenry reacts with concern. Today, we are in such a period of concern.

By successfully crafting settlement policy, however, the government can shift attention to the value of immigrants. For the most part, the government has left to private institutions the process of immigrant settlement. This privatized response, however, has become more difficult since the society has expanded its responsibilities to all residents. Selectively, the United States has chosen to exclude non-naturalized immigrants from some (permanent residents) or all (the undocumented) of these benefits. It has not supplemented this selective exclusion, however, with a conscious policy of settlement, so that immigrants can develop an interest in membership in the United States and acquire the skills to accomplish this end.

The success or failure of these efforts will contribute to the ultimate dilemma posed by immigration to the contemporary United States. In the past, the nation has incorporated immigrants as individuals. Should this effort begin to fail, immigrants could come to believe that they are being excluded as a group from the dominant society. They may, then, decide to make demands as a group for rights or for political inclusion. It is likely that U.S. society would react quite negatively to such group-based demands. Such demands, however legitimate, would raise concerns about immigration that would spur society to lose its fondness for immigrants.

5

Immigrants Versus Immigration: Structuring the Discussion of Dilemmas in Immigration, Naturalization, and Settlement Policy

I'm convinced that when the second boatload of
pilgrims landed in Massachusetts, those on the
Mayflower said "There goes the neighborhood."

—Ben Wattenberg, quoted in Thomas J. Espenshade
and Maryann Belanger, "U.S. Public Perceptions
and Reactions to Mexican Migration"

FROM EARLY IN THE NATION'S HISTORY, though perhaps not quite as early as columnist Ben Wattenberg pithily observes, the United States has had a contradictory approach to the engine of its own population growth. Immigrants are revered, whereas the aggregation of the immigrant experience—immigration—is treated with much more caution and often outright opposition. When we introduced this contradiction at the beginning of Chapter 2, we indicated that the course of U.S. *policy* has been to facilitate immigration through most of the nation's history. The exceptions, however, have been stark. Periods of mass mobilization in opposition to immigration have led to significant, if in some cases short-term, changes in policy. Because we may be entering just such a period now, we conclude our study by examining the outlines of popular perceptions toward immigration. We then put these popular concerns in the context of the dilemmas that we have identified in U.S. immigration, naturalization, and settlement policy.

Popular Perceptions of Immigrants and Immigration

The majority of Americans oppose immigration at current levels (Espenshade and Belanger 1997). Survey data from mid-1995 indicate that approximately two-thirds of U.S. adults believe that current levels of immigration should be reduced. Just 7 or 8 percent of adults, however, believe that immigration should increase.

Attitudes Toward Current Levels of Immigration

The public makes distinctions among types of immigration, both in terms of legal status and national origin. In the area of legal status, the general public mistakenly believes that the majority of immigrants are undocumented. Two-thirds of respondents in a 1993 Gallup survey, for example, expressed this opinion. However, the scholarly consensus is that undocumented immigrants account for no more than 30 percent of the annual immigrant flow. Regardless of the actual numbers, this perception of an uncontrolled border shapes popular views about immigration. This is evident from a 1993 survey that asked whether immigration was a serious problem. Approximately 15 percent of respondents said that the presence of legal aliens in the country concerned them "a great deal." The presence of undocumented immigrants, however, concerned 48 percent "a great deal."

Popular concern about the volume of immigration causes people to distinguish among the national origins of immigrants. A 1995 Gallup poll, for example, found that 56 percent of Americans felt there were too many immigrants from Latin America, but only 44 percent felt there were too many Asian immigrants.

Thus, not only are Americans broadly opposed to the current levels of immigration, they also have some sense that not all immigrants are the same. Scholarly research indicates that some of these popular perceptions are wrong (for example, concerning the proportion of all immigration made up of undocumented immigrants), but this recognition of the complexity of immigration demonstrates that popular opposition is tempered by an understanding that some immigration is necessary and desirable.

Popular Attitudes Toward Immigrants

As we have indicated, immigrants earn greater popular respect than does immigration. Again, this respect is tempered by where immigrants come from and whether they are legal or undocumented. In 1993, Gallup conducted a poll examining attitudes toward eight national-origin groups. The majority of the respondents reported that four of these national-origin groups—Chinese, Koreans, Irish, and Poles—contributed more to the society than they took (see Table 5.1). For the other four national-origin groups—Mexicans, Cubans, Haitians, and Vietnamese—the popular perception was that the problems they created exceeded the benefits they produced. Although this poll focused on countries and not regions, it reinforces the finding that Americans are more resistant to Latin American immigration at current levels than they are to Asian and European immigration.

The same poll examined national attitudes toward traits that are often associated with immigrants—work ethic, competitiveness, interest in school, and family values. These responses illustrate the contradictory popular attitude toward immigration and immigrants. On three of the traits, the majority of respondents view immigrants positively, perceiving that they have strong family values, are hardworking, and are not too competitive (see Table 5.2). On the fourth trait, the majority of respondents reported that Asian immigrants do well in school but were evenly split over whether Latin American immigrants do so. Again, these results reinforce the finding that Americans are more resistant to Latin American immigration at current levels than they are to Asian and European immigration.

Thus, popular concern about the volume of contemporary immigration has not altered a basic respect for the immigrants themselves. The polling data cannot

TABLE 5.1   Perceptions of Immigrant Benefits and Immigrant Costs, by National Origin, 1993

Immigrant Contribution	*Mexicans (%)*	*Cubans (%)*	*Haitians (%)*	*Chinese (%)*
More benefits	29	24	19	59
More problems	59	64	65	31
Both	5	3	2	2
No opinion	7	9	14	8

Immigrant Contribution	*Koreans (%)*	*Vietnamese (%)*	*Irish (%)*	*Poles (%)*
More benefits	53	41	75	65
More problems	33	46	11	15
Both	3	3	3	2
No opinion	11	10	11	18

Source: Gallup Organization poll of 1,002 adults, conducted in October 1993, quoted in Espenshade and Belanger 1997:242–243.

tell us how individuals balance these contradictory feelings. In practice, they may never have to be balanced for most individuals. Instead, government institutions establish balance by creating and enforcing restrictions on immigration while facilitating the entrance of immigrants with popularly respected and needed traits. This process appears from the first restrictions on immigration in the late nineteenth century, which controlled potential immigrants with disliked behavioral and ideological traits, to today's efforts to facilitate the immigration of family members, professionals, and those with needed labor skills. Although these conflicting attitudes toward immigration and immigrants can be maintained at the individual level, they cannot so easily be maintained at the level of government. As a close reading of our discussion of immigration, naturalization, and settlement should suggest, mass and elite attitudes in these policy areas often vary. Whereas the mass interests have long shown the opposition to immigration evident in the data presented in this chapter, the history of U.S. immigration policy reveals that these restrictionist impulses have rarely been dominant in U.S. policy.

The current wave of popular concern about the level of immigration and the quality of some of the immigrants that are being admitted is not unique in American political history. Instead, there have been at least four such periods before at the national level and an uncountable number in localities, states, and regions. These previous waves of popular concern spurred national legislative efforts to

TABLE 5.2   Perceived Characteristics of Immigrants, 1993

Trait: Do Very Well in School		
	Latin America (%)	Asia (%)
Applies	42	74
Does not apply	42	17
No opinion	16	9

Trait: Have Strong Family Values		
	Latin America (%)	Asia (%)
Applies	72	77
Does not apply	19	16
No opinion	9	7

Trait: Are Hardworking		
	Latin America (%)	Asia (%)
Applies	65	74
Does not apply	27	20
No opinion	8	6

Trait: Are Too Competitive		
	Latin America (%)	Asia (%)
Applies	26	40
Does not apply	64	52
No opinion	10	8

Source: Gallup Organization poll of 1,002 adults, conducted in October 1993, quoted in Espenshade and Belanger 1997:246–248.

control naturalization at the end of the eighteenth century, unsuccessful legislative efforts to achieve the same goals in the mid-nineteenth century, and the development of an international bureaucratic structure to set qualifications for admission as a legal immigrant and to restrict access to those who do not meet these qualifications in the 1920s. Once these mechanisms were in place, public concern spurred the enactment of restrictive qualifications that survived for approximately forty years, restrictions that limited the number of immigrants and prevented the immigration of those who were culturally very different from the majority of the U.S.-born population. The final wave of public concern, which began in the mid-1970s and focused originally on the undocumented, has had a less obvious result. In response, Congress enacted an elaborate regulatory structure to reduce the rewards of undocumented immigration. Yet it also enacted loopholes and failed to assure sufficient resources for implementation. Thus, this current wave of popular concern has had a less obvious impact and offers the foundation for today's popular opposition to immigration.

If this popular opposition to immigration recurs, why has U.S. policy so continuously favored large-scale immigration and naturalization opportunities for some or all immigrants? The first part of the answer is undoubtedly a function of the basic contradiction in popular attitudes. Average Americans may oppose immigration, but their attitude toward individual immigrants is more positive. Thus, even during periods when popular opinion in the United States strongly opposes immigration, individual immigrants usually find a receptive environment.

Second, immigration is rarely a salient issue for most Americans. In surveys that do not raise specific questions about immigrants, few respondents (no more than 1 or 2 percent) volunteer a statement that immigration is a particularly important issue either for the nation as a whole or for their community. Instead, issues such as economics, crime, and morality are much more likely to be volunteered as important issues.

This, then, demonstrates the third factor that has facilitated the continuing openness of the United States to immigration and naturalization. Elite consensus has more consistently supported immigration. In part, this elite consensus is driven by organized interests in the society such as manufacturers and agricultural concerns that benefit from a large workforce. Immigrant labor provides more than just person power. In some sectors of the economy, traditionally those requiring the fewest skills, they allow employers to pay low wages. Thus, manufacturers and agricultural interests have had a consistent interest in immigration, but they are not alone. Early in the nation's history, states and territories in the Midwest and West demanded immigrants to populate the land. Today, universities benefit from the immigrant flow, to fill graduate classrooms and laboratories that the U.S.-born population cannot fill. Some high-tech industries also depend on immigrant labor. Although this list is not exclusive, it suggests a foundation for the ongoing demand for immigration by elites within the society. For these key sectors of the economy, immigration is always highly salient. As a result, their concerns are more often met than those of the general population, which may regard immigration negatively but most of the time is not too concerned about it.

The foundation, then, of U.S. immigration policy is somewhat tenuous. This, we believe, explains why the dilemmas that we have identified in the text are largely ongoing throughout American history and cannot be finally resolved. When popular opposition mounts, immigration, naturalization, and settlement policies are subject to change. A dramatic reversal has not occurred at the national level since the 1920s, though efforts to limit the employment opportunities of the undocumented can be seen as a failed national effort to reshape an aspect of this policy. However, the various renewed state efforts to reinvigorate their role in policymaking in this area indicate that federal immigration policies may not represent all views.

Dilemmas in the Shaping of Immigration, Naturalization, and Settlement Policies

We conclude with a brief review of the dilemmas that we have identified in the shaping of immigration, naturalization, and settlement policy. Broadly, these dilemmas can be understood as a continuing national effort to shape the characteristics of immigrants and immigration.

1. Chapter 2. Immigration: How many immigrants should the nation admit, and what characteristics should they have?
2. Chapter 3. Naturalization: Which immigrants should be incorporated as citizens, and on what terms should they be incorporated?
3. Chapter 4. Settlement: What is the legal relationship between immigrants and the U.S.-born, and how does this relationship structure the settlement of immigrants?
4. Crosscutting dilemma in immigration, naturalization, and settlement policy: What level of government should design and implement immigration, naturalization, and settlement policy?

The dilemma concerning immigration is straightforward, though highly contentious: How many immigrants should the nation admit, and what characteristics should they have? Over the past two hundred years, the nation has developed rules that define whether any person is eligible to immigrate. The nation has also tried, less successfully, to establish goals for the number of immigrants who should be admitted in a given year. These rules, however, have remained contentious because, in a sense, they are rules for what America will become. Changes in immigration today lead to a different ethnic mix in future years. Historical efforts to restrict immigration to the populations that have immigrated in the past have galvanized popular opinion but have never succeeded for long, in large part because of the continuing demand for immigrant labor. As a result, the dilemmas that we have identified as characterizing past debates about immigration policy will likely continue as long as the policy remains to admit large numbers of immigrants.

The continuing dilemma in naturalization policy has proved less vexing for the United States: Which immigrants should be incorporated as citizens, and on what terms should they be incorporated? Although knowledge-based requirements have been added in the twentieth century, the basic outline of what is required of naturalizing citizens remains remarkably similar to the requirements throughout most of the two-hundred-year history of the naturalization program. The opportunity to naturalize has also expanded, from "free white males" to all nationalities. To the extent that history provides a cue, it is likely that the standards will increase incrementally in the future but that naturalization will remain accessible to all immigrants who seek to become U.S. citizens.

As the government has taken on more responsibilities in the twentieth century for providing a social safety net, the dilemma identified in Chapter 4 has emerged in discussions of immigrant policy: What is the legal relationship between immigrants and the U.S.-born, and how does this relationship structure the settlement of immigrants? The role of the government in shaping immigrant policy may seem noncontentious on the surface, but the questions raised in Chapter 4 demonstrate how this question of governmental responsibility is very much in debate. Although this question may not have been too important in the nation's early days, it has become steadily more important as the role of the state in assisting individuals has grown. Increasingly, we would predict, the conflict between mass and elite interests over immigration that the nation has seen in the past will take the form of debates over the rights and privileges of immigrants. In this regard, short-term interests, such as those expressed by California voters in 1994 or by Congress in the 1996 changes to programmatic benefits, may impede the nascent efforts to create an immigrant settlement policy in the United States.

Underlying each of these dilemmas is the question of federalism in immigrant and immigration policy. In Chapter 2, we examined what level of government should control immigration policy and, equally important, what level of government should enforce these restrictions on immigration. In Chapter 3, we assessed what level of government should administer the transition from denizen to citizen. In Chapter 4, we examined the role that states are seeking to play in the allocation of rights and privileges to immigrants and to the establishment of a settlement policy. Although the federal government has steadily limited state powers in the making and implementation of immigration and naturalization policies, the federalist structure of government in the United States assures that the states will assert themselves when the federal government fails to act, as in its policy toward undocumented immigration.

Conclusion

We began our study by highlighting a simplified model that explored the transition from immigrant to citizen. As the intervening discussion should have suggested, there is no direct connection between these two points. Instead, immigrants may choose to become citizens, or not. Similarly, the government may facilitate this transition, or not. As we have indicated in this chapter, the shaping of these dilemmas is influenced by an ongoing tension between mass concerns about immigration and greater levels of elite support for it. With these concerns in mind, it is important to note that most of U.S. history has been characterized by large-scale immigration. Thus, to the extent that history is a guide, immigration will continue to be a part of American life, though undoubtedly in different forms. This prompts a final lesson. The discussion of naturalization and settlement that has traditionally received far less attention by scholars and policymakers will become of increasing importance to the society. The success or failure of the political and social incorporation of today's immigrants depends in part on increased national attention not just to whom the United States admits but also to what the country offers these immigrants once they are here.

Study Questions

Chapter One

1. What are some of the factors that spur emigration and immigration?
2. What are the differences between the following categories of immigrants to the United States—permanent residents, undocumented immigrants, tourists, refugees, and asylees?

Chapter Two

1. Oscar Handlin has argued that the history of America is the history of the immigrant. What is the basis of this argument? Do you agree with his contention?
2. What differentiates the immigrants in each of the four eras of immigrant history? Are there common patterns that appear across these four eras of immigration to the United States?
3. What were the barriers faced by the U.S. government when it first sought to establish limits to immigration? Who was newly excluded from immigration between 1865 and 1921? Why?
4. Who immigrates to the United States today? Where do these immigrants come from, and on what basis do they establish their eligibility to immigrate? How do the economic and social opportunities of today's immigrants compare to those of turn-of-the-century immigrants?
5. How has Congress tried to control undocumented immigration? What policy options has it not tried in order to enforce immigration laws?

Chapter Three

1. Why does the Constitution vest control of naturalization in the federal government? What would the consequences have potentially been if naturalization rules could be established by each of the states?
2. What are the requirements for naturalization, and when was each requirement enacted?
3. What is birthright citizenship? Why does the United States grant citizenship to all children born in its territory? What are the arguments in support of birthright citizenship, and what are the arguments against it? Should the children of immigrants have this right?
4. Why did the federal government take the authority to administer naturalization away from the states and localities? How did federal administration change the implementation of naturalization laws?
5. Among contemporary immigrants, who naturalizes and who does not? Why?

Chapter Four

1. How do the rights, privileges, and responsibilities of non-naturalized immigrants differ from those of U.S. citizens?
2. What is the justification for denying noncitizens voting rights, employment and occupational privileges, and programmatic privileges?
3. In what areas have the states tried to assert control of the settlement process? What are their objectives? Do you think that state involvement will speed or hinder the process of immigrant settlement?
4. Why have programs targeted at racial or ethnic minorities often been extended to cover immigrants? Do you think that this extension of minority programs to immigrants will speed or hinder the process of immigrant settlement?

Chapter Five

1. Based on the discussion not just in Chapter 5 but throughout the book, why have mass and elite interests often differed on immigration policy? Under what circumstances are mass opinions translated into policy?

Glossary

Alien and Sedition Acts (1798)   Legislation enacted by Federalists in Congress to control a perceived threat to U.S. national security. The acts tried to control naturalization by extending the period of residence prior to citizenship to fourteen years and centralizing control over its award. Reversed in 1802, the Alien and Sedition Acts were strongly partisan and represented the last grasp for power by Federalists prior to the rise of the Jeffersonian Democrat Republicans.

American, or "Know-Nothing," Party   A political party that emerged in New England in the early 1850s. The party included anti-immigrant rhetoric as part of its platform. Its immigration-related focus was naturalization (the concept of immigration control did not yet exist). It sought to extend the period prior to naturalization to twenty-one years, in part as a tool to control the voting power of the Irish and German immigrants who began to appear in large numbers in the 1840s. The party was known as "Know-Nothing" because its members defined themselves as being pure Americans, i.e., as not knowing anything beyond core American values.

Asylee   A person not resident in his or her country of citizenship who cannot return to that country based on a fear of persecution. Asylees, like refugees, present problems for policymakers in that most countries find it difficult to establish standards for what forms of persecution merit admission as an asylee.

Chinese Exclusion Act (1882)   This legislation barred immigration from China and the naturalization of Chinese immigrants. The Chinese Exclusion Act began a process of exclusion of immigration from all of Asia and naturalization of Asian immigrants that was not reversed until 1952.

Citizen   A person with full political rights, privileges, and responsibilities in a society.

Civil Service Requirements   Progressive reformers sought to reduce the power of the political machines by making public employment more professional and less subject to patronage. Civil service systems required that job applicants demonstrate skills for the job they were seeking and protected jobs during changes in the government's elected leadership.

Contributory Programs   Governmental programs that award a programmatic benefit based on the level of an individual's contribution. People who contribute more receive a greater benefit. Social Security provides an example of this type of program.

Coolies   The popular term used to refer to Asian contract laborers. Arguing that contract labor, particularly contract labor from Asia, was a new form of slavery, Congress terminated immigration eligibility for coolies in 1875—one of the first restrictions on immigration.

Denizens   Residents of a country who are not citizens of that country.

Deportation   The removal of an immigrant from a country. Although formal deportation from the United States requires a legal proceeding, many undocumented immigrants voluntarily depart and never subject themselves to deportation.

Diversity Visas   A new category of preference immigrant visa established in the 1990 Immigration and Nationality Act. These visas are available to nationals of countries that historically sent a large number of immigrants to the United States but that have not been able to under the family preference provisions of the 1965 Immigration Act. Immigrants from English-speaking countries also have special access to diversity visas.

Electoral College   Presidential elections in the United States are indirect. Voters elect members of the Electoral College (electors), who then elect the president. The authors of the Constitution designed this indirect system to reduce the influence of popular passions on the selection of the president.

Ellis Island   The island in New York Harbor used to process immigrants in the late nineteenth and early twentieth centuries. Symbolically, Ellis Island and the Statue of Liberty, which stands on another island near Ellis Island, represent immigration of this era in the popular mind.

Emigration   The movement out of a country.

Employer Sanctions   A provision in the Immigration Reform and Control Act of 1986 that made it a crime to knowingly employ an undocumented immigrant. To comply with IRCA, employers must verify each new employee's work eligibility within the first two days of work. Employers must complete an I-9 form and indicate what form of proof of citizenship or work eligibility the employee offers. The employer must then keep these I-9 forms and provide them to Immigration and Naturalization Service inspectors if asked.

Enclaves   Immigrant and ethnic neighborhoods that are partially self-sustaining. Immigrants and ethnics work for, buy from, rent from, and interact economically with other immigrants from the same country or with coethnics. Successful enclaves are rare—the Cubans in Miami and the Chinese in San Francisco offer examples. When they develop, however, they offer a tool for immigrant and ethnic economic development.

English-Only Movement   A political movement in the 1980s and 1990s to prohibit the use of languages other than English in the delivery of government services. The movement calls for state and local statutes and an amendment to the U.S. Constitution to accomplish this goal. The movement began in Florida in response to Dade County's efforts to deliver services to Cuban immigrants in Spanish and has become national in scope.

Entitlement Programs   Governmental programs in which the level of benefit is not determined annually. Instead, a preexisting formula determines future spending. Although Congress can change this formula, beneficiaries have an expectation of future benefits and often believe that they are entitled to this benefit level; and they therefore react negatively to efforts to reduce the benefit formula.

Family Unification   In the Immigration and Nationality Act of 1965, family unification offers the most common form of visa allocation. Although this has changed slightly in the 1990s, the 1965 act established largely unrestricted immigrant eligibility for immediate family members of U.S. citizens (spouses, minor children, and parents) and more restricted immigrant eligibility for collateral relatives of U.S. citizens (siblings and adult children) and immediate relatives of permanent residents.

First Papers   Between 1795 and 1952, immigration law required that three years before applying for naturalization, immigrants file a Declaration of Intention to naturalize. This declaration, called "first papers," was used by many states around the turn of the century to determine the point at which immigrants gained eligibility to vote.

First- and Second-Generation Immigrants   We use these terms to refer to immigrants (first generation) and their U.S.-born children (second generation). Some analysts use the term "first generation" for both the immigrants and the first U.S.-born generation.

Fourteenth Amendment (1868)   The second of the post–Civil War constitutional amendments. Extending equal protection to all citizens (including the former slaves), the Fourteenth Amendment also granted citizenship to children born in the United States (except for the children of diplomats).

Franchise   The vote. Notions of who in the society is entitled to the franchise have shifted over time. Initially, only property holders had the franchise. By the 1830s, it became a right of all white male adults. With the Fourteenth and Fifteenth Amendments, African Americans formally gained the franchise, though it took another one hundred years for this formal guarantee to reach the mass of African-American adults. In the twentieth century, women and those eighteen to twenty years old achieved the franchise through constitutional amendment.

Great Potato Famine   A disease in Ireland killed most potato plants, the main form of nutrition of Ireland's poor (the impact was felt only among the poor; other classes did not subsist on potatoes). The famine killed over 1 million people between 1845 and 1851 and spurred the first huge migration to the United States.

Great Society   The package of social safety net programs enacted during the administration of President Lyndon Johnson (1963–1969). Among these programs were those for health, such as Medicare and Medicaid, for education assistance, such as Head Start, and for assistance to the elderly, such as Supplemental Security Income.

Illegal Immigrants   (see Undocumented Immigrants).

Immigration   The movement of people into a country.

Immigration and Nationality Act of 1965   The immigration legislation that replaced the National Origin Restrictions of the 1920s. The 1965 act enshrined family unification and labor migration as the central elements of eligibility for immigration. The rapid growth in immigration in the last three decades is the result of the family unification provisions of this law.

Immigration Reform and Control Act (IRCA)   Passed in 1986, this bill sought to control undocumented immigration to the United States. The bill included three major elements—employer sanctions, legalization, and Special Agricultural Workers. Employer sanctions established penalties for the employment of undocumented workers and required employers to ascertain the legal status of all new employees. Legalization provided that undocumented immigrants who had been resident for approximately five years or longer could become permanent residents. Special Agricultural Workers offered an assurance to agricultural interests that they would have sufficient labor. These three elements reflect the compromise nature of the bill. With the exception of the legalization program, the bill is viewed as a failure.

In re Rodríguez (District Court for the Western District of Texas, May 3, 1897)   In this case, the federal courts established that immigrants from Mexico were eligible for naturalization under the laws of the day, which allowed naturalization of "free white persons" and immigrants of African nativity. The court reasoned that since citizenship had been extended to the former Mexican residents of the Southwest after the Mexican American War in 1848 when only whites were eligible to become U.S. citizens, Mexicans must be white.

Indentured Laborers   People who trade their labor for a set period of time for the price of transit. During the early period of immigration to the colonies, indentured servants made up a majority of immigrants. The ease of fleeing the contract once in the colonies, however, reduced the appeal of this form of labor to landholders seeking labor. Today, indentured servitude has returned among some undocumented immigrants, particularly those from Asia.

Initiative   A process by which citizens can initiate a measure to be put on the state electoral ballot. If passed, these initiatives have a force of law subordinate only to the state constitution and thus can only be reversed by another initiative or a constitutional amendment.

Involuntary Immigrants   People transported internationally against their will, such as slaves.

Jus Solis   Award of citizenship to individuals born within a given territory. Advocates of *jus solis* understand nationhood to be a voluntary association of individuals within a state. The children of these people who are engaged in a voluntary association, then, are also entitled to membership in the state.

Labor Recruitment   Organized efforts to encourage an individual or group to migrate with the promise of a job in a specific industry or region of the United States. Labor recruitment often taps migrants from immigrant-sending areas that had not previously sent immigrants to the United States and can, thus, create a new stream of migrants to the United States.

Legalization   A program that awards permanent resident (legal) status to immigrants in an undocumented status. The most recent large-scale legalization occurred as part of the Immigration Reform and Control Act of 1986. Approximately 2 million formerly undocumented residents of the United States became permanent residents under provisions of the program. Many are today eligible to naturalize as U.S. citizens.

Migration   Movement of people from one place to another.

National Origin Restrictions (or Quota Acts)   The first major restriction on immigration to the United States. Enacted initially in 1921 and strengthened in 1924, these laws sought to limit overall numbers of immigrants and to allocate visas within the lower overall numbers to immigrants from Northern and Western Europe. This legislative goal was accomplished by allocating visas based on the share of each European ancestry group in the 1910 census and the 1890 census (in the 1924 act). This legislation, which was the model for U.S. immigration law until 1965, met the goals of its authors. The number of immigrants declined and the share of Southern and Eastern Europeans dropped. The National Origin Restrictions are important for a second reason. In order to enforce these acts, the United States had to establish an international system under which visas were issued abroad and the immigrant's eligibility to live permanently in the United States was verified prior to emigration.

Naturalization The process by which an immigrant earns full rights within the receiving society. The United States today requires five years of residence (or three, if the person is married to a U.S. citizen who has been a citizen for the full three years); ability to speak, read, and write English; and knowledge of U.S. history and civics. As we indicate, the ability of the immigrant to negotiate the bureaucracy proves an equally important, though not a formal, requirement.

Needs-Tested Governmental programs that allocate benefits based on having income below a designated level. All people whose personal or family incomes fall below the designated level are entitled to the programmatic benefit.

New Deal The period of social reform and response to the Great Depression during the first two terms of President Franklin Roosevelt's administration (1933–1941). The New Deal established social insurance programs such as Social Security and direct assistance programs such as Aid to Mothers (now Families) with Dependent Children that laid the foundation for the federal social welfare safety net that has been developed over the past sixty years.

Operation Hold the Line A border control strategy developed and implemented in El Paso in 1994. Instead of trying to capture the undocumented once they are in the United States, Operation Hold the Line sought to prevent people from crossing the border in the first place by having border patrol agents within sight of each other along the border twenty-four hours a day. This strategy is expensive because of personnel costs. Although it deters short-term crossers going to El Paso, its impact on long-term undocumented immigration is less clear since migrants can go around the border patrol. A similar strategy was subsequently implemented in San Diego and at other major border-crossing cities along the U.S.-Mexican border.

Permanent Residents Immigrants who have entered the United States under the provisions of the immigration law with the right to remain in the United States. For most of the nation's history, after five years, permanent residents have been eligible to naturalize as citizens. As long as they remain primarily resident in the United States, permanent residents may remain noncitizens for the rest of their lives.

Plyler v. Doe (457 U.S. 202 [1982]) The federal courts ruled that undocumented immigrant children have a constitutional right to education. The nature of the ruling and changes in the membership of the Supreme Court have led some to believe that the courts might be open to reversing the ruling in *Plyler v. Doe*. To date, there has been no such ruling; *Plyler* offered the constitutional justification for holding the educational provisions of California Proposition 187 unconstitutional.

Preference Immigrants   Categories of potential immigrants who are allocated a specific number of visas each year, for example, siblings of U.S. citizens or spouses of permanent residents. The number of these visas is limited, and there is often a multiyear backlog to obtain one. The waiting list is so long for some from high immigrant-sending countries that the visas are simply not available.

Private Sector   Business and other nongovernmental parts of the economy.

Progressive Era Reforms   In the first three decades of the twentieth century, political reformers known as Progressives sought to reduce the power of the urban political machines. They proposed a series of electoral reforms—including personal registration requirements, the secret ballot, the establishment of a professional civil service, and primary elections. Over time, these were successful in reducing the power of the machines. In the process, the reforms reduced the political resources available to immigrant communities that traded the votes to the machine for crude social services and patronage jobs.

Proposition 187   A ballot proposition passed by California voters in November 1994 that calls for the exclusion of undocumented immigrants from public social services and health care services, the exclusion of undocumented immigrants and their children (regardless of citizenship status) from public elementary and secondary schools, the exclusion of undocumented aliens from public colleges and universities, the criminalization of the manufacture or use of false citizenship or resident alien documents, and the promise of added cooperation between state agencies and the Immigration and Naturalization Service. Opponents of Proposition 187 sought and received an injunction against its implementation. In November 1997, a federal judge held most of Proposition 187 to be unconstitutional finding that it usurped federal responsibility over immigration policy.

Public Sector   The government, in the federal, state, and local spheres.

Quota Acts   (see National Origin Restrictions).

Radical Republicans   Congressional leaders in the period just after the Civil War. The Radical Republicans sought full citizenship rights for the freed slaves and punitive measures against Southern states.

Refugee   A person who emigrates in the face of immediate persecution or violence in his or her home country. Most countries find it difficult to establish standards for what forms of persecution merit admission as a refugee. Often, ideological standards and foreign policy considerations prove more important than the gravity of the threat of violence.

Registry (1929)   Congress established this program to legalize the status of immigrants who could prove they had been resident in the United States since 1921. The program has been updated several times. Today, undocumented immigrants who can show they have been resident in the United States since 1972 can legalize their status and become a permanent resident.

Remedial Programs Government programs designed to redress past discrimination. Affirmative action programs, for example, seek to remedy past discrimination against African Americans, Latinos, Asians, and Native Americans by offering added opportunities today.

Settlement The process of transition from immigrant to citizen. Settlement can be facilitated or inhibited by state policies that encourage or discourage attachment to the new country and economic and social adaptation. Unlike other contemporary immigrant-receiving countries, the United States does not have a comprehensive settlement policy.

Sojourners Short-term residents of the United States who intend to return to their home countries. Many analysts of immigration have assumed that immigrants are sojourners and have no loyalty to the United States. In practice, however, most immigrants develop an attachment to the United States quite rapidly, so few immigrants are true sojourners.

Sponsor The U.S. citizen, permanent resident, or company that petitions for the immigration of a foreign national. Formally, the sponsor takes financial responsibility for the immigrant. This responsibility has been largely voluntary. Legislation passed by Congress in 1996, however, made the sponsor's responsibility legally binding and tied any social welfare use by the immigrant to the income of the sponsor plus that of the immigrant.

Undocumented Immigrants Immigrants who do not have the authorization of the immigration law to enter or remain in the United States. Undocumented immigration is only possible when the law excludes some immigrants from eligibility to immigrate. Thus, for practical purposes, undocumented immigration did not exist in the United States until the 1920s. Estimates in the mid-1990s indicate that there are 5 million undocumented immigrants in the United States.

Urban Political Machines The political organizations that controlled urban politics in most large Eastern and Midwestern cities in the second half of the nineteenth century and the first part of the twentieth century. These machines often relied on immigrant votes to maintain power and were controlled either by immigrants or their children. In exchange, the machines offered a crude system of social welfare, some jobs, and, most important, assistance with settlement and adaptation to the United States. The reforms promoted by the Progressive movement (as well as declining immigration beginning in the 1920s) began to end the power of the urban political machines in most cities.

Voting Rights Act of 1965 This legislation gave teeth to the requirement in the Fifteenth Amendment that states not abridge citizens' voting rights. The 1965 act mandated that Southern jurisdictions not impede efforts of African Americans to register and vote. It also transferred judicial proceedings concerning voting rights in these states to Washington, D.C., and provided for federal monitors to protect African Americans trying to register and vote. The act was amended and expanded in 1970, 1975, 1982, and 1992.

References

Altman, Ida, and James Horn. 1991. *"To Make America": European Emigration in the Early Modern Period*. Berkeley and Los Angeles: University of California Press.

Alvarez, Robert. 1987. "A Profile of the Citizenship Process Among Hispanics in the United States." *International Migration Review* 21 (2) (Summer):327–351.

Anbinder, Tyler G. 1992. *Nativism and Slavery: The Northern Know-Nothings and the Politics of the 1850s*. New York: Oxford University Press.

Balderama, Francisco E., and Raymond Rodríguez. 1995. *Decade of Betrayal: Mexican Repatriation in the 1930s*. Albuquerque: University of New Mexico Press.

Barkan, E. R., and N. Khokolov. 1980. "Socioeconomic Data as Indices of Naturalization Patterns in the United States: A Theory Revisited." *Ethnicity* 7:159–190.

Brubaker, Rogers. 1992. *Citizenship and Nationhood in France and Germany*. Cambridge: Harvard University Press.

Calavita, Kitty. 1992. *Inside the State: The Bracero Program, Immigration, and the I.N.S.* New York: Routledge.

de la Garza, Rodolfo O., and Louis DeSipio. 1993. "Save the Baby, Change the Bathwater, and Scrub the Tub: Latino Electoral Participation After Seventeen Years of Voting Rights Act Coverage." *Texas Law Review* 71 (7) (June):1479–1539.

———. Forthcoming. "Interests Not Passions: Mexican American Attitudes Toward Mexico, Immigration from Mexico, and Other Issues Shaping U.S.-Mexico Relations." *International Migration Review.*

DeSipio, Louis. 1996. *Counting on the Latino Vote: Latinos as a New Electorate*. Charlottesville: University Press of Virginia.

DeSipio, Louis, and Rodolfo O. de la Garza. 1992. "Making Them Us: The Political Incorporation of Culturally Distinct Immigrant and Non-Immigrant Minorities in the United States." In *Nations of Immigrants: Australia, the United States, and International Migration*, edited by Gary Freeman and James Jupp, 202–216. Melbourne: Oxford University Press.

Erie, Steven P. 1988. *Rainbow's End: Irish Americans and the Dilemma of Urban Machine Politics*. Berkeley: University of California Press.

Espenshade, Thomas J., and Maryann Belanger. 1997. "U.S. Public Perceptions and Reactions to Mexican Migration." In *At the Crossroads: Mexico and U.S. Immigration Policy*, edited by Frank D. Bean et al., 227–262. Lanham, MD: Rowman and Littlefield Publishers.

Espenshade, Thomas, and Katherine Hempstead. 1996. "Contemporary American Attitudes Toward U.S. Immigration." *International Migration Review* 30 (2) (Summer):535–570.

Fuchs, Lawrence H. 1990. *The American Kaleidoscope: Race, Ethnicity, and the Civic Culture.* Hanover and London: Wesleyan University Press.

García, John A. 1981. "Political Integration of Mexican Immigrants: Explorations into the Naturalization Process." *International Migration Review* 15 (4):608–625.

_____. 1987. "Political Integration of Mexican Immigrants: Examining Some Political Orientations." *International Migration Review* 21 (2):372–389.

Gavit, John Palmer. 1971 [1922]. *Americans by Choice.* New York: Harper Brothers Publishers.

Guest, Avery. 1980. "The Old-New Distinction in Naturalization: 1900." *International Migration Review* 14 (4):492–510.

Handlin, Oscar. 1951. *The Uprooted: The Epic Story of the Great Migrations That Made the American People.* Boston: Little, Brown and Company.

Immigrants' Welfare. 1996. Vol. 1, no. 1 of Research Perspectives on Migration. Washington, DC: International Migration Program of the Carnegie Endowment for International Peace and the Urban Institute.

Jasso, Guillermina, and Mark Rosenzweig. 1990. *The New Chosen People: Immigrants in the United States.* New York: Russell Sage Foundation.

Muller, Thomas. 1992. *Immigrants and the American City.* New York: New York University Press.

NALEO (National Association of Latino Elected Officials). 1986. *Proceedings of the First National Conference on Citizenship and the Hispanic Community.* Washington, DC: NALEO Educational Fund.

_____. 1988. *New Citizens in Limbo: One in Three Applicants Neither Pass nor Fail.* Washington, DC: NALEO Educational Fund.

_____. 1991. *Rejection of U.S. Citizenship Applicants: One Out of Four Applicants Bureaucratically Rejected Annually.* Washington, DC: NALEO Educational Fund.

National Immigration Law Center. 1994. *Guide to Immigrant Program Eligibility.* Los Angeles: National Immigration Law Center.

North, David S. 1985. *The Long Grey Welcome.* Washington, DC: NALEO Educational Fund (reprinted in abbreviated form in *International Migration Review* 21 [2]:311–326).

Pachon, Harry P., and Louis DeSipio. 1994. *New Americans by Choice: Political Perspectives of Latino Immigrants.* Boulder: Westview Press.

Pear, Robert. 1993. "U.S. to Encourage Legal Immigrants to Get Citizenship." *New York Times,* November 26.

Portes, Alejandro, and John Curtis. 1987. "Changing Flags: Naturalization and Its Determinants Among Mexican Immigrants." *International Migration Review* 21 (2):352–372.

Portes, Alejandro, and Rafael Mozo. 1985. *Latin Journey: Cuban and Mexican Immigrants in the United States.* Berkeley: University of California Press.

Rosberg, Gerald. 1977. "Aliens and Equal Protection: Why Not the Right to Vote?" *Michigan Law Review* 75 (April-May):1092–1136.

Sánchez, George P. 1993. *Becoming Mexican American: Ethnicity, Culture, and Identity in Chicano Los Angeles.* New York: Oxford University Press.

Schuck, Peter H., and Rogers M. Smith. 1985. *Citizenship Without Consent: Illegal Aliens in the American Polity*. New Haven: Yale University Press.

Seller, Maxine Schwartz. 1988. *To Seek America: A History of Ethnic Life in the United States*. Rev. and enlarged. Englewood, NJ: Jerome S. Ozer Publisher.

Tomás Rivera Center. 1996. *The Latino Vote at Mid-Decade*. Claremont, CA: Tomás Rivera Center.

U.S. Bureau of the Census. 1993a. *Statistical Yearbook of the United States 1993*. Washington, DC: U.S. Government Printing Office.

————. 1993b. *The Foreign-Born Population in the United States. 1990 Census of Population*. 1990CP-3-1. Washington, DC: U.S. Government Printing Office.

U.S. Immigration and Naturalization Service. 1992. *1991 Statistical Yearbook of the Immigration and Naturalization Service*. Springfield, VA: National Technical Information Service.

————. 1993. *1992 Statistical Yearbook of the Immigration and Naturalization Service*. Springfield, VA: National Technical Information Service.

————. 1994. *1993 Statistical Yearbook of the Immigration and Naturalization Service*. Springfield, VA: National Technical Information Service.

————. 1996. *1994 Statistical Yearbook of the Immigration and Naturalization Service*. Springfield, VA: National Technical Information Service.

————. 1997. *1995 Statistical Yearbook of the Immigration and Naturalization Service*. Springfield, VA: National Technical Information Service.

U.S. Senate, Committee on the Judiciary. 1980. *History of the Immigration and Naturalization Service*. Washington, DC: Congressional Research Service.

Wolfinger, Raymond, and Steven Rosenstone. 1980. *Who Votes?* New Haven: Yale University Press.

Wyman, Mark. 1993. *Round-Trip to America: The Immigrants Return to Europe, 1880–1930*. Ithaca: Cornell University Press.

Yang, Philip Q. 1994. "Explaining Immigrant Naturalization." *International Migration Review* 28 (3):449–477.

Index